A
LEADER
AFTER GOD'S
OWN HEART

JIM GEORGE

HARVEST HOUSE PUBLISHERS

EUGENE, OREGON

Cover by Garborg Design Works, Savage, Minnesota

A LEADER AFTER GOD'S OWN HEART
Copyright © 2012 by Jim George
Published by Harvest House Publishers
Eugene, Oregon 97402
www.harvesthousepublishers.com

Library of Congress Cataloging-in-Publication Data
George, Jim, 1943-
A leader after God's own heart / Jim George.
    p. cm.
ISBN 978-0-7369-3700-9 (pbk.)
ISBN 978-0-7369-4501-6 (eBook)
1. Leadership—Religious aspects—Christianity. 2. Nehemiah (Governor of Judah) I. Title.
BV4597.53.L43G46 2012
253—dc23
                                                            2011038497

Printed in the United States of America.

            12 13 14 15 16 17 18 19 20 / BP-SK / 10 9 8 7 6 5 4 3 2 1

CONTENTS

An Invitation to Godly Leadership

Leadership is a vast and almost impossible subject to capture within the confines of a 200-page book. Just go to your local bookstore, either Christian or secular. In every case, you'll find multiple shelves devoted to this important topic. Every field of endeavor has its secrets for those who aspire to positions of prominence. The business community has its formulas for leadership, as do the political and media communities. And for sure, you and I as Christians also have our instructions—from Scripture—on what's involved in becoming a leader.

For me, learning about leadership had its beginnings in my local church. Sure, I had been to the bookstore and bought scores of books about leadership. Also, as a pharmaceutical salesman, I had personally observed my bosses and their examples of leadership. But all that pales in comparison to the valuable and life-changing principles for leadership that were based on the Bible and taught in the church I attended. This was the launching pad for my leadership development and eventually my becoming a leader in a local body of believers.

In my church, God provided strong and visible models of godly leadership. And as I read my Bible, I was blessed by the examples of great leaders like Abraham, Joseph, Moses, Joshua, and David. The flesh-and-blood examples within the covers of my own Bible provided great insight into the subject of leadership. And one man in particular, Nehemiah, has fascinated me over the decades that I have studied leaders and leadership.

Nehemiah was, in many ways, just an ordinary guy who was going about his business when God reached down and asked him to step up and be a leader for Him. And because you've taken the initiative to read this book, the same is probably true about you. Either you are already a leader, or perhaps God is reaching down and asking *you* to step up and become one.

If you are willing to accept God's challenge, then this book will provide guidance on how you can become a strong leader through which God works in other people's lives.

Because the Bible is silent about much of Nehemiah's life, I have included in this book many observations that have been drawn from Bible commentaries, books on manners and customs in Bible times, and other kinds of historical texts.

In addition, I have tried to imagine the problems the leader Nehemiah ran up against, and what he might have thought or felt with each challenge he faced. I tried to envision the Bible scenes describing Nehemiah's situations, and use those texts to paint a portrait of this amazing man and leader. I have tried to get into his mind—and his soul—as he sought to be a leader after God's own heart. I have tried to put you and me right there in Nehemiah's day and in Nehemiah's sandals. I wanted you to hear his heart, experience his problems, and observe—up close and personal—how he successfully resolved his issues and led God's people.

It is my prayer that the "15 Ways to Lead with Strength" presented in this book and demonstrated by Nehemiah will provide a model for how you, too, can strengthen your leadership in your sphere of life. May your leadership be based on God's Word and empowered by His Spirit—and may you become *A Leader After God's Own Heart*.

In Him,
Jim George

Part 1:

The Call to Strong Spiritual Leadership

1

STRENGTH...GOD'S PROMISE FOR YOUR LEADERSHIP

*I can do all things
through Christ who strengthens me*
(PHILIPPIANS 4:13).

The moment of truth had arrived. Nehemiah's career—even his very life—flashed before his eyes. *What was I thinking?* he wondered as he was forced into a reality check. *What made me ever dream I could fool others, especially those I serve and work with so closely?*

Nehemiah had prayed for an opportunity like this. But when it came without a warning—or even a hint—he was caught so completely off guard that his heart and mind flooded with fear in an instant. However on the fringe of this emotion, faith began to flicker and kindle and ignited its way into his soul. Faith worked its strengthening miracle, and he began to remember who he was.

Yes! Nehemiah's heart began to remind him. *I am the cupbearer to the king. I am one of the most trusted men in the Persian Empire. I am one of a select few the king allows into his presence. I have rank and privilege. I serve the king!*

The king's cupbearer felt his strength and confidence gaining momentum. And then he recalled the real reason for this moment. *I am answering my God's call to serve Him.* And yet, in that instant, he hesitated and wondered, *How will my earthly—and highly unpredictable and volatile—king react to what I'm about to ask? To what I must ask?*

Nehemiah's Backstory

Before we see the king's response to the burning question Nehemiah was forced to ask his sovereign, let's turn back the pages of time some four months. To the Hebrews it is the month *Chislev* (which translates to November-December on our calendar). The scene is Susa, the winter capital of the immense Persian Empire, which spans all the way from Egypt to India. Our story and the making of a leader after God's own heart begins with what appears to be a biography—or maybe even an autobiography—of a man named *Nehemiah*, meaning "Jehovah comforts."

Nehemiah's story begins without fanfare. There are no trumpets, no crowds, and no pomp and circumstance. There is no introduction, no genealogy, no ta-da. That's why most scholars believe that Ezra, the scribe, a contemporary of Nehemiah, was probably the author of the book that relates Nehemiah's story and reveals the making of a leader. If Nehemiah had written this chronicle himself, he, like most other autobiographers, would have included more background details, and surely more personal information, don't you think?

The opening verse of the book of Nehemiah tells us this man was "the son of Hachaliah." We know little to nothing about Hachaliah. And the only other bit of information Ezra shares in chapter 1, verse 1 is that Nehemiah was the king's cupbearer.

Doesn't sound like much, does it? No big deal—at least in today's culture. Are you picturing Nehemiah as a waiter at some fancy restaurant? Or maybe a butler? Well, don't. There's certainly nothing wrong with these professions, but back in 445 BC, holding the title *cupbearer* was something special—*very* special.

A cupbearer was much more than a servant. He was more like a personal assistant. He held a position of great privilege and responsibility. And what he did was risky! At each meal, the cupbearer tested the king's wine to make sure it wasn't poisoned.

And there's more. Because this man, the cupbearer, stood close to the king in public, he had to be handsome, cultured, and knowledgeable in court procedures. To top off his job qualifications and requirements, he had to be able to converse with the king and advise him if asked to do so. Because a cupbearer had such access to the king, he was considered an important official of great influence—influence he could use for good or evil.

And there's even more. Nehemiah wasn't just *a* cupbearer to the greatest ruler of his day. No, he was *the* cupbearer! This distinction may have made him *the* most trusted and significant man in the employment of the king of Persia. So, when Ezra reported that Nehemiah was "the cupbearer to the king," this was truly a big deal!

At this point, maybe you are wondering, *How did Nehemiah end up becoming a super-trusted guy in the greatest kingdom of his day?* The scribe Ezra gives us very little to go on. He records scarcely anything about Nehemiah's origins and rise to power. So we're curious. Did Nehemiah inherit his privileged position, like so many leaders do? Or did he pay a large sum of money to secure this position, like so many leaders do? There are no answers. The author leaves these matters to our imagination.

Because we know so little about our soon-to-be hero's rise to power, and because our subject is leadership and the strength it requires, perhaps we would find it more beneficial to explore this from a different angle: What made Nehemiah the man of the hour when the king needed to choose someone to become his trusted confidante? His almost coleader? His personal assistant? A team member? His bodyguard at least when it came to a willingness to sacrifice himself for the king's life as his wine tester? Or, what qualities did Nehemiah exhibit—qualities revealed throughout the book of Nehemiah—that contributed to his being such a strong leader?

If you've wondered about the qualities that make for a strong leader, you'll find them present in Nehemiah's life. In this book, you'll explore these traits and discover how you can make them a part of your life. If you've desired to grow in your leadership abilities yet haven't been sure of how to make that happen, this book will help you to start setting specific goals for growth and begin living out the potential God has placed in you. You can move out boldly, with strength, in your personal quest to be a leader after God's own heart.

Who, Me? A Leader?

Maybe you've struggled in the past with the whole matter of whether you are even called to be a leader. When you look at the greats of the Bible—men like Abraham, Moses, David, and Nehemiah—you wonder if you could ever measure up. You want to be used by God, but maybe you've felt you just don't have what it takes. Or maybe you're not even quite sure you *want* to be a leader!

Well, put your qualms and questions to rest. The call to serve as a leader is not confined to the elite ranks of the greats in the Bible. Nor is it restricted to CEOs or CFOs of a company. The term *leader* is not reserved only for those who chair committees at your church or stand in the pulpit. There are many situations in which a man is needed to provide leadership.

Mark it well—*every man is to see himself as a leader*. God calls each of His men to be leaders, and that includes you. He expects you to be a leader, whoever you are, wherever you are, and whatever your job or profession. In your home. In your family. In your dorm. In your military unit. On your team. At the workplace. God wants to use you—yes, *you*—as a powerful voice for Him.

To be useful, then, you must see yourself as God does—as a leader, or at least a leader in the making. So accept the challenge. Shift into leadership gear. And throttle forward. God wants you to move out toward the magnificent plans He has for you and the mighty ways He wants to use you. And to start the process rolling, God has given you a model in Nehemiah. And He's also given you promises in His Word that, in Him, you already have the strength to fulfill the challenge!

God's Power Team

One evening I was surfing through the TV channels looking for my favorite program, The Weather Channel. That's when I caught a glimpse of The Power Team, and backed up to take a closer look. I had heard about these big guys before, but I'd never seen them in action. So I took a few minutes to get a better understanding of their outreach ministry.

In case you haven't heard of The Power Team, it's made up of a group of ex-jocks and bodybuilder and military types who tour the country and share their testimonies about what it means to have faith in Jesus Christ. These guys are incredible! They perform various feats of strength, such as breaking huge blocks of concrete with their bare hands. They are a team of Christian men who use their physical strength to entertain while they speak about their love for Christ and the spiritual strength He gives them.

But these men are not the only guys who can be on a "power team." If you know and love Jesus, you too are assured of God's provision of strength. Where can you get some of this divine power that you need to be God's kind of man, His kind of leader? Here's the answer…and a promise of what God wants to do for you:

> *I can do all things*
> *through Christ who strengthens me*
> (PHILIPPIANS 4:13).

Now, let me quickly state that when you appropriate this promise of God's strength, you probably won't be able to break huge blocks of concrete into pieces. Rather, tapping into God's kind of strength will empower you to be victorious in all areas of the Christian life. That's way better than breaking cement blocks, don't you think?

Understanding the Promise

What a promise! "I can do *all things* through Christ who strengthens me." Now, what are some of the "all things"?

1. Strength in Every Circumstance

The triumphant words of this promise come from the apostle Paul. And his confident reference to "all things" has to do with being in control in every circumstance. So, whether Paul possessed a little or a lot, or whether he suffered a little or a lot, he was able to handle it, whatever "it" was. His I-can-do-all-things attitude was the same in every circumstance and condition (see Philippians 3:12).

Do you have any issues, any problems, any lacks, any "its" and "things" to deal with in your life? As a leader of a few or many, of those at home or elsewhere, this has to be a rhetorical question. Men of God are *always* faced with difficult problems and issues! So read on as Paul tells you how he made it through "all things."

The promise—The first half of this "power verse" declares a truth: "I can do all things," or "I can do all this" (NIV). This is the kind of message you would expect to hear from a motivational speaker or a coach. It conveys the idea of self-reliance and self-assurance. It says, "*You* can do it! *You* can do anything you want to do if you put your mind to it."

Statements like these may be true in some areas of a person's life, and to some extent it is true that, with enough determination and willpower, you can accomplish a lot. But when you consider the *source* of such power, that's not what this verse is saying. So you have to read on and finish Paul's message: He reveals that you "can do all things *through Christ*," who strengthens you!

The source—You can't miss it: Christ is the source of the strength mentioned in Philippians 4:13. Don't pass over this important truth—it's *Christ* who makes this happen. *He* is the reason you can do "all things" in the spiritual realm. How was Paul able to have this kind of optimistic perspective on all of the issues of life? It was because of Christ, who was Paul's power source, who is also your power source.

How often have you tried to handle some aspect of your life in your own strength and abilities? You had the skills. You had the know-how. Maybe you even had the human resources—the time and the money. But you tried to go it alone. You tried to go it without considering or involving the Lord. You tried to do it yourself. Well, how did that go for you?

I can make a pretty good guess. That's because I've been there and done that! I'm guessing you probably got the job half done… or maybe you even failed miserably. God's message is loud and clear—stop trusting in your own strength and abilities, and start relying on Christ and His strength instead.

2. Strength for Purity

There are many topics and issues we could discuss that require Christ's strength to overcome. Right away you could list physical health, problems related to your job, the lack of together-time with family, a shortage of money. But sexual purity seems to be The Big One for many men. Keeping your mind and body sexually pure is, as the title of a popular book indicates, *Every Man's Battle*.

Purity is a challenge. It's a daily struggle, and yes, a daily battle. But as Scripture clearly states, purity is God's will for you: "This is the will of God, your sanctification; that you should abstain from sexual immorality; that each of you know how to possess his own vessel in sanctification and honor, not in passion of lust" (1 Thessalonians 4:3-5).

How then can you as a Christian man, as a leader, stay pure? The answer is simple yet powerful: *I can do all things through Christ who strengthens me.*

If purity is a source of struggle for you (and don't forget—the book title mentioned above included the word *every*), remember one thing: Draw on the source of all strength. Draw on the power of Jesus Christ and fight your battle. Draw on the power of the Holy Spirit for self-control. You *can* do all things, even win the battle over sexual temptation, if—and only if—you allow Christ to give you His supernatural strength to overcome the temptations that are bound to come up along the way.

3. Strength for Christian Living

And so it goes! No matter what challenge you face, or what circumstances or temptations arise (and arise they will), God promises that you can do all things through Christ and His strength. Christ's power is sufficient for any and all areas of your life, period. What are some of the other struggles you face? What about being...

- a growing Christian?
- a loving and supportive spouse?
- a caring parent or grandparent?
- a faithful steward of God's resources?
- a helpful friend?
- a committed student or employee?
- a humble servant?
- a witness for Jesus?

Do you think God wants any or all of these qualities to be true about you? You know the answer, don't you? It's an absolutely resounding *yes*! God desires that you do all of the above—and more. Therefore, God has given you Jesus Christ and promises you that His strength will empower you to accomplish His will.

Putting God's Power to Work

So let's say you desire God's strength in your life. Now what? The following steps will get you started down the path of putting God's power—the power He's already provided—to work in you.

Abide in Christ

Jesus put it this way: "I am the vine, you are the branches; He who abides in Me, and I in him, bears much fruit; for without Me you can do nothing" (John 15:5). In the same way that a branch must stay attached to a vine so it can bear fruit, to receive power from Christ, you must stay closely connected to Him. If your union with Him is strong, then the power of God will infuse and strengthen you to successfully face and manage challenges that come your way. As you abide in Christ, you will have strength for today's trials as well as for all of tomorrow's challenges. Do whatever you must to stay close to the Power Source and the Source of All Power: Read your Bible daily and pray faithfully. Stay connected! Abide in Christ.

Exercise Your Faith

How do you grow in physical strength? By exercising your body. And this principle is also true in the spiritual realm. You grow in spiritual strength by exercising your faith daily when you…

- trust God for the needs in your life
- pray and look for God's answers
- rely on God's strength in your weaknesses
- believe God's promises in your every trial
- live as a consistent witness of your beliefs
- stand up for your faith

Develop a Positive Attitude

You've heard it before: "Attitude is everything!" Having the right attitude is fundamental to being an effective leader. Everyone enjoys being around a person who is helpful and searches for solutions. A positive attitude also looks for the good in everything instead of the bad. And why *shouldn't* you have a positive attitude? You are a soldier in the army of the King of kings. You "can do all things through Christ." And how is that possible? Because it is Christ who strengthens you (Philippians 4:13).

Be Accountable to Others

If your commitment to Jesus Christ, the Power Source, starts to flicker and wane, you will be powerless to handle the challenges and temptations that come your way and demand your best self. And come they will! What's one solution? To team up with other godly men. They can help you to protect your devotion to Christ and waylay any chances of your drifting away from Him. Surround yourself with godly Christians. Find spiritual mentors who will check up on you, especially in the areas where you struggle.

Nehemiah on Leadership

Nehemiah didn't have the power of the indwelling Holy Spirit, which you have as a New Testament and church-age follower of Jesus Christ. But he did believe in the powerful God of Israel. As a student of the Old Testament law and prophets, he knew the history of God's faithfulness in fulfilling His promises. Nehemiah's strength of leadership was based on his belief in the same type of promise God gave to Joshua, an earlier leader and general of God's army. God told Joshua:

> Be strong and of good courage; do not be afraid, nor be dismayed, for the LORD your God is with you wherever you go (Joshua 1:9).

Nehemiah was truly an amazing man! But he was just a man—like you. What set him apart? What made him a leader after God's own heart? He forged an iron-like faith in God. He was consistently positive. He focused on what needed to be done: He challenged the people of Israel, "Let us build the wall of Jerusalem" (Nehemiah 2:17). And he trusted God and looked to Him for His promised strength:

> Those who trust in the LORD will find new strength. They will soar high on wings like eagles. They will run and not grow weary. They will walk and not faint (Isaiah 40:31 NLT).

Friend, you can be on God's Power Team—on God's team of powerful leaders! You can trust God's promise that you "can do all things through Christ," who strengthens you. Now, it's up to you to exercise your faith in Christ and act on this powerful truth.

PART 2:

The Traits of Strong Spiritual Leadership

CRISIS MANAGEMENT...
DRAWS OUT YOUR LEADERSHIP

Hanani one of my brethren came with men from Judah;
and I asked them concerning the Jews
who had escaped, who had survived the captivity,
and concerning Jerusalem
(NEHEMIAH 1:2).

Who knew? It was the dawning of a pleasant winter day sometime during November or December 446 BC. As Nehemiah woke up that morning, he was in no way prepared for what he would face later in the day. As usual, he made his way from his apartment through the maze of halls and stairs that led to the king's chambers in his magnificent winter residence in Susa. Nehemiah was about to begin his daily duties as cupbearer to Artaxerxes, the feared and powerful king of Persia.

As Nehemiah quietly and efficiently performed his responsibilities, a servant arrived, bowed low, and delivered a message. It was a note informing him that his brother, Hanani, had just arrived from Jerusalem. Nehemiah turned and glanced back at the king, taking care to hide his excitement.

When there came a pause in his routine, Nehemiah respectfully asked permission from King Artaxerxes to be excused for a few minutes to take care of a personal matter. Thankfully, the king sensed no hint that anything unusual was taking place. And he hadn't noticed any change in Nehemiah's demeanor. So he waved his trusted cupbearer out of the room.

Out of sight, Nehemiah shifted into high gear. He hurried through the halls and navigated the stairs, trying hard to remember to retain the dignity his office demanded.

His mind was racing too. He didn't even need to wonder, *How long has it been?* No, Nehemiah knew *exactly* how long—it had been 13 years. It had been 156 months. It had been 624 weeks. That's how long it had been since Nehemiah had seen his beloved brother. That's how long it had been since he had last heard from Hanani. It felt like forever. News had been by rumor only…for 13 long years.

Nehemiah was filled with eager anticipation as he hurried to meet with his long-lost brother. His heart yearned to look upon and embrace his childhood companion. And he was anxious to hear a report about the welfare of God's people and the condition of the city of Jerusalem. He was eager for proof of how God had answered his 13 years of prayers and supplication that the Lord would restore His people and bring His city back to its rightful glory. He relished a firsthand account from Hanani's own lips, not to mention an opportunity to catch up with all that was taking place in Hanani's life and enjoy comradery with him.

As he quickened his pace, Nehemiah continued calculating the outcome his brother would surely report: *With the 50,000 people who returned with Zerubbabel some 90 years ago, and then Ezra's return with more than 7000 people 13 years ago, the region should have recovered nicely from its devastation by the Babylonians 160-plus years ago. We must celebrate! We must give thanks to God.*

But no. As his brother came into view, Nehemiah was appalled at how weathered and defeated he looked. What Hanani had experienced had aged him beyond his years. *Oh no! Is it possible that conditions in Jerusalem are so severe that they have taken such a toll on my brother?* As Nehemiah kept closing the distance between him and Hanani, his curiosity turned into anxiety as he noticed the deeply troubled look on Hanani's face.

"Hanani, my brother! Shalom to you," Nehemiah said as he gave his sibling the traditional Oriental greeting, a kiss. And then, before Hanani could answer with his own greeting, Nehemiah followed up with his questions of concern...not at all sure he really wanted to hear the answers.

While there is no record that confirms whether this was the scene that played out between Nehemiah and Hanani, it is quite possible that their encounter was along these lines. However it unfolded, the arrival of Hanani and his men signaled the arrival of a crisis.

The Arrival of a Crisis

A crisis is an event, a happening, or a situation that often becomes a critical occurrence or turning point in a person's life. A crisis can be either physical, mental, emotional, or spiritual. The issue is not the "happening" itself—life is made up of many happenings. The issue is how you as a person—and especially as a leader—deal with the crisis *when* and not *if* it comes. So the real question is, How do you deal with the happenings in your life?

Some people handle a crisis by running from it, avoiding it, ignoring it, deflecting it. By becoming compromised by it, or destroyed by it.

Then there are those who respond positively to a crisis. They accept it. They face it. They use it. They learn from it. And then they grow from it. The late President John F. Kennedy made this observation: "When written in Chinese the word *crisis* is composed of two characters. One represents danger and the other represents opportunity."[1] This raises a question that gets to the heart of crisis management: Do you see a crisis as a danger, or as an opportunity?

As we continue to walk with Nehemiah, we will see that he is about to face a crisis. He is in the employment of a powerful ruler over a pagan empire. He has a good job. No, he has the greatest of jobs! He is trusted by the king and lives in the king's palaces. Why would anyone want to jeopardize the dream job of a lifetime? Nehemiah wasn't a soldier or a priest. He was just a private citizen. He could easily divorce himself from any involvement with the concerns of Jerusalem. But he didn't. He cared about the people and their struggles. So, what should he do? What *would* he do?

Nehemiah's Role in Crisis Management

Life is not easy for anyone. More than once I've heard this saying used among US Navy SEALS: "The only easy day was yesterday"— meaning today is going to be hard, so you might as well face it head-on. Living through each day boils down to making it through the current crisis. And better than merely getting *through* it is *managing* it. That's the mark of real leadership: A leader has an ability to manage a crisis correctly.

We've already defined a crisis as a "happening." Simply put, it's an event, a happening, or a situation that brings about a crucial turning point in someone's life. And usually it's something challenging, or even undesirable. It is at the very moment when a crisis hits that you must decide how your special set of circumstances should be handled. Do you ignore it? Or do you deal with it?

So how did Nehemiah rise to the occasion and take on the role of a crisis manager? And did he see the crisis as a danger, or an opportunity?

Nehemiah's first response was one of concern for the people: "I asked them concerning the Jews who had escaped, who had survived the captivity" (1:2). That is, he asked how things were. His brother, Hanani, and others answered, "The survivors who are left from the captivity in the province are there in great distress and reproach" (verse 3).

Then they explained one of the reasons the people were under such deplorable conditions: "The wall of Jerusalem is also broken down, and its gates are burned with fire" (verse 3).

Let's pause for a minute to fill in the historical details of what had taken place. Jerusalem and its walls were destroyed by the Babylonians in 585 BC. In spite of repeated attempts to rebuild the city, it still lay in ruins 160-plus years later. Without a wall to protect them, God's people were defenseless. Bandits could come upon them and attack without warning and carry off their food and supplies—and even carry off some of the people into slavery.

Because Jerusalem's walls were in ruins, the Jewish people became known as the "city-without-walls people"—they lost status in the eyes of the other nations. They were seen as a small, pathetic group. And even worse was the humiliation they felt because they were unable to protect themselves.

How did Nehemiah, a leader after God's own heart, respond to such gut-wrenching news?

He showed a deep concern for the people. Normally the SNL (Strong Natural Leader) has it the other way around. He—the SNL—is more concerned with the *things* under his control. He will ask, "Was any equipment damaged?" Or, "How will this affect our reputation in the marketplace?" And ultimately, "How will this affect our bottom line?"

Only secondarily does a SNL ask, "Was anyone hurt?" Or, "How will this merger or closure affect the lives of the employees?"

The authors of the book entitled *In Search of Excellence* state that excellent companies live a people orientation. They treat people as adults, as partners, as important resources."[2]

The renowned British historian Sir Arthur Bryan also affirms this attitude in successful leaders. He states, "No one is fit to lead his fellows unless he holds their care and well-being to be his prime responsibility, his duty…his privilege."[3]

A moment of reflection: You are probably not getting ready to rebuild a wall and save a nation. But you do have your own set of crises that require a lot of your attention.

How's your home today? Your home life? If you are a husband and father, you have plenty of opportunities to lead as you manage the myriad of happenings that occur in your family. The people under your roof should be your first priority and concern. Here's a self-test: Am I taking care of my family unit the way I should be? And, How can I be more involved and visible in showing my concern for my family and the issues my wife and kids are dealing with on a daily basis?

And what about the people at your workplace? Are you at all interested in your fellow workers? Are you a team player? Or are you thinking only of yourself and what's best—or easiest—for you? Next to your family, the welfare of your co-workers should appear near the top of your concern list. You need to ensure you are doing your job so they can do theirs. You need to understand that it's only when these people are free from personal anxiety that they can function better both at home and on the job. You don't have to be the one who frees them of these anxieties. But you *can* be the one who points them in a better direction or shows them a better way.

When you care about the people around you, you're practicing strong leadership.

Responding to a Crisis

A willingness to manage a crisis to the best of your ability is a mark of true leadership. Any person can do nothing. That's easy. But a leader will always step up and do something to deal with the crisis at hand. While he might not always handle a situation 100 percent correctly, he will at least make an attempt to find the best possible solution.

What steps can you take to enjoy success in dealing with your present crisis and the crises that are sure to come—whether it involves building (or rebuilding) a wall around Jerusalem, or handling an issue at work or on the home front? Read on!

Step #1: *Ask questions*—If you don't know the facts involved, you might mishandle a crisis. But as you ask questions and gather answers, you will better comprehend the extent of the crisis and what needs to be resolved. That's what Nehemiah did—he first asked about the people. A leader after God's own heart is always interested in the hearts and welfare of God's people. Then he asked about the walls. Armed with answers, he had the information he needed to begin managing the crisis.

Step #2: *Listen*—Nehemiah began his fact-gathering efforts by providing a sincere listening ear. He wanted a firsthand report of all the facts. By contrast, most people begin the leadership process with their mouth. Many leaders aren't really all that interested in hearing from others. They're too busy giving out marching orders even before it's been decided which direction to march toward! In his book *The Top Ten Mistakes Leaders Make*, Hans Finzel points out that one of the signs of a "paper pusher" rather than a "people worker" is that the paper pusher "listens poorly—if at all."[4] Obviously, a people worker makes an effort to listen.

Step #3: *Seek help*—No crisis is wholly unique. Certain aspects of any given crisis have occurred before. As King Solomon put it, "That which has been is what will be, that which is done is what will be done, and there is nothing new under the sun" (Ecclesiastes 1:9). But it is also true that each crisis arrives with new twists and turns. For these new challenges, a leader seeks help. Again, as King Solomon, the wisest man who ever lived, said:

> Where there is no counsel, the people fall; but in the multitude of counselors there is safety (Proverbs 11:14).

> Without counsel, plans go awry, but in the multitude of counselors they are established (Proverbs 15:22).

A good leader will seek the wisdom of others. After all, no man is an island! Therefore, a smart leader surrounds himself with a corps of wise counselors. He knows a leader is only as wise and as capable as his advisors. A Christian leader has three sources of counsel: First, he has God's wisdom as revealed in God's Word, the Bible. Second, he has the wisdom of good counselors. And third, he has the wisdom of the Holy Spirit as he seeks guidance through prayer.

Scripture doesn't reveal whether Nehemiah consulted God's Word—he probably did. Nor does it say he sought the wisdom of others—he probably did this as well. But we do know from the Bible that Nehemiah did take the third path to wisdom—he sought resolution of the crisis through prayer. While we won't look at Nehemiah's prayer life until the next chapter, we can know that he was not about to proceed until he had consulted God through prayer.

Step #4: *Determine a strategy*—Based on the counsel he receives, a leader makes a decision and chooses an appropriate way to deal with a crisis. In the upcoming chapters we'll see that Nehemiah determined he would be part of the strategy. He asked God for guidance…and God chose *him* to be part of the solution to avert the crisis!

Step #5: *Implement and monitor the progress*—Here's a sneak preview: Soon you will see Nehemiah's response to the crisis. You'll see him choose to go to Jerusalem himself. You'll see him become part of implementing a plan and monitoring its progress and completion. You'll see him elect to personally be a part of turning the crisis around—a crisis that had been in the making for at least 90 years!

As you read the continuing saga of Nehemiah's stunning leadership and his decision to personally go and assist in the rebuilding of the city of Jerusalem, you'll see crisis after crisis rising up to challenge the strength of this leader after God's own heart, this leader who longed to see the fortifying walls secure around God's city. And with each crisis, you'll see Nehemiah go through the process of determining how best to proceed. You will witness him making wise choices as each crisis and curveball is handled successfully. And you will begin to realize why Nehemiah is such a sterling study in the art of leadership.

A Comparison of Two Different Responses

A Modern-day Success in Crisis Management

Now fast-forward 2500 years. It's fall. The year is 1982. A murderer coldheartedly decides to add 65 milligrams of cyanide to some bottles of Tylenol capsules on store shelves. This act killed seven people, including three in one family. Now, *this* is a crisis—a killer crisis!

What did the makers of Tylenol do? The leadership of Johnson & Johnson recalled and destroyed 31 million capsules, costing their company $100 million. The company's CEO made it a point to appear in television ads and at news conferences to inform consumers of the Johnson & Johnson's actions: Tamper-resistant packaging was rapidly introduced, and Tylenol sales swiftly bounced back to near pre-crisis levels.

A Modern-day Disaster in Crisis Management

Seven years after the Tylenol crisis, on March 24, 1989, a tanker belonging to the Exxon Corporation ran aground in Prince William Sound in Alaska. The Exxon Valdez spilled millions of gallons of crude oil into the waters off Valdez, killing thousands of fish, fowl, and sea otters. Hundreds of miles of coastline were polluted, and salmon spawning runs were disrupted. Numerous fishermen, especially Native Americans, lost their livelihood.

Exxon, in contrast to Johnson & Johnson, did not react quickly in terms of dealing with the media and the public. In fact, the company did not appoint a public relations manager to its management team until 1993, four years after the incident. At that time Exxon established its media center in Valdez, a location too small and too remote to handle the onslaught of media attention. From then and there, the company acted defensively in its response to the public, even laying blame, at times, on other groups such as the US Coast Guard. As I am writing this book, the crisis is still ongoing, some 20-plus years later.

NEHEMIAH ON LEADERSHIP

As you survey your personal and professional life, and read and view the news on a daily basis, you know all too well that no sector of life is immune from crises. Whether it's the family crisis where you make a dash to the emergency room when little Johnny falls out of a tree and breaks his leg, or the business crisis you face when there's a significant drop in sales revenues, or the personal crisis when you lose your job or your health, crises are a fact of life.

Pause for a minute and think back over this past week. How many different problems did you encounter? A lot, right? You should never be surprised at the number of disrupting events you must deal with. The fact your crises are a real and constant part of everyday living makes it all the more important to do well at crisis management.

That's why there's great benefit in looking at how Nehemiah handled the many crises that came his way. We can already learn from his example in the way he responded upon learning about the desperate situation in Jerusalem and among God's people. We are to respond hopefully and prayerfully, with God's wisdom and strength. And more specifically, Nehemiah's actions teach us the following:

> *Don't ignore a crisis.* A crisis, by its very nature, requires attention. That's why it's called a crisis. Nehemiah faced his crisis head-on.

> *Don't deflect a crisis.* A leader deals with a crisis. And, like Nehemiah, a leader may at some point need—and ask for—help. But he first assesses the crisis and determines what part he can and must play in managing it.

> *Don't shift blame for the crisis.* The issue is not *who* caused the problem. It's *what* can be done to turn the crisis around. Once the crisis has been handled, its cause can then be determined and corrected.

> *Don't overreact to a crisis.* It's probable that a medical crisis should be handled quickly. But beyond that, as a general rule, don't make hasty decisions in response to a crisis. Most issues don't graduate to crisis-level overnight. So take the time you need to make sure you respond wisely.

Do respond by determining the extent of the crisis. Get the
   facts. Listen without judgment until you have enough
   information to begin formulating a solution.

Do seek the advice of others. There is much wisdom in counsel. Like Nehemiah, make sure you seek the wisdom of
   others, and the direction of God through prayer.

Nehemiah was an influential man before he was aware of the
crisis in Jerusalem. He was already a man after God's own heart.
But, with the Jerusalem crisis came the opportunity to function at
a higher and more significant level of leadership. Nehemiah didn't
know it, but God was about to use him to rebuild the walls around
the city of Jerusalem. And once the walls were in place, Nehemiah's
remarkable leadership would make it possible to reestablish worship and purify God's people. All this happened because one man
was strong enough to respond in the right way to a crisis.

What crisis are you facing today? This week? How is God wanting you to respond and deal with it? Accept the challenge. Allow
God to draw out the hidden leader in you through your demanding situation. Learn to lean on Him for strength and wisdom. Live
out this observation made by J. Oswald Sanders:

> *It would not be exaggeration to affirm that never*
> *in human history have leaders been confronted*
> *with such a concentration of unresolved crises and*
> *impossible situations as in our day. Consequently,*
> *if they are to survive, they must be able to thrive*
> *on difficulties and regard them as routine.*[5]

3

PRAYER...EMPOWERS YOUR LEADERSHIP

"O LORD, I pray, please let Your ear be attentive
to the prayer of Your servant,
and to the prayer of Your servants
who desire to fear Your name; and let Your servant
prosper this day, I pray, and grant him
mercy in the sight of this man."
For I was the king's cupbearer
(NEHEMIAH 1:11).

Prayer had never been a last resort. Oh no, not for Nehemiah! When it came to prayer, his motto was, "Others may, I cannot." His daily thought was, *Others may skip prayer here and there, talk to God now and then, or fail to pray altogether...but I cannot!* So, like many other devout Jews of his day, and following in the steps of the great statesman before him, Daniel, Nehemiah spent time each day facing toward the west—in the direction of Jerusalem—and praying.

Nehemiah had always had a deep respect for and a sense of the significance of the city of Zion. And he had prayed all those years for the safety of the brave souls who had made the 1000-mile journey back to Jerusalem. But on this particular day, as Nehemiah came to his chambers and once again opened his windows toward Jerusalem, things were different—drastically different! Today he had heard distressing news. His heart was broken. His mind was bewildered. It appeared that God's affairs, God's name, and God's glory had advanced very little, even after more than 140 years of effort. Unbelievable! In fact, it seemed from today's reports that just the opposite had occurred: God's name and God's people were a reproach!

What can I do? Nehemiah's heart cried out.

There was only one thing Nehemiah could do. It was what he had always done. He could pray.

As he fell to his knees, he opened his heart and his mouth to appeal to God's character and covenant. He beseeched the one true God to intervene and fulfill His pledge to His chosen people. From the center of his soul, Nehemiah's impassioned plea poured forth:

> I pray, LORD God of heaven, O great and awesome God, You who keep Your covenant and mercy with those who love You and observe Your command-ments, please let Your ear be attentive and Your eye open, that You may hear the prayer of Your servant which I pray before You now, day and night (Nehemiah 1:5-6).

Must-have Qualities for Leadership

If you are feeling like you've just stepped on holy ground, you have. Through God's inspired written Word, you and I have just entered into prayer alongside Nehemiah. He's a leader. And he's a leader with a problem. And, as a leader after God's own heart, he knows how to lean on God's strength for all that it takes to live by and lead toward God's purposes. He knows to look to God first—then lead others. He knows too that a life of prayer and a dependence upon prayer is a must-have quality in a leader. He also knows that as a leader of others, he must first and foremost be a prayer warrior.

Recently I found on the Internet an informative list of qualities for successful leadership. Its title? *Twelve Characteristics of a Great Leader.* Since you are reading this book—a book on leadership—you have probably already seen many other publications with similar lists. If you're shopping in a grocery store that carries books and magazines, they are there. If you're traveling through an airport, you'll see them there too. If you're browsing in a bookstore or searching on the Internet for resources and information on leadership, such lists are there. So I'm thinking as you read this list drawn from this article, you will agree that the author has captured many of the characteristics necessary for being a good leader. They are all important and essential:

1. Leaders are always improving. They understand that things are changing around them. They also understand that for them to be a leader they must be changing too!

2. Leaders inspire the people around them to become better. People want to do their best because of their leadership.

3. Leaders know how to concentrate on people's strengths, not their weaknesses. Everyone has something they excel at, and a good leader knows how to bring this out in a person.

4. Leaders are proactive, not reactive. They recognize the importance of leading their people and not waiting for somebody else to get started.

5. Leaders treat people with respect and importance. They know that to get someone to do something, that person needs to want to do it.

6. Leaders are self-motivated. They know there will be ups and downs in life and in their business. But they stay positive, not allowing outside influences to affect their attitudes.

7. Leaders work on communicating. They learn how to say the right thing at the right time.

8. Leaders are prepared. They don't leave things to chance, but rather control situations through preparation.

9. Leaders don't have big egos. They care about others instead of being self-centered.

10. Leaders are mentors. They see the importance of mentoring others and know how to pass on the knowledge they have attained.

11. Leaders have written goals. And they strive to achieve them. They understand the necessity of goal setting and the example they are setting.

12. Leaders are hard workers. They never expect more out of the people around them than they are willing to give themselves. This type of attitude is contagious and motivates others to make a greater effort.[6]

The author's final assessment is also true: "If you strive hard to do these 12 things you yourself can become a great leader as well."[7]

Wow—what a gem of a list! Goals set and progress made in these 12 areas would incite us toward becoming better leaders. But from a biblical perspective, did you notice one key element missing from the list—maybe *the* key element? In a word, *prayer*.

If you've already read other books and articles on leadership, you've probably noticed that many of them don't mention prayer as being important in the life and effectiveness of a leader. To the average SNL—Strong Natural Leader—the demonstration of religious faith and the need to pray—even the idea of prayer—is a sign of weakness. Some might even say that prayer has no place in leadership, that it's an unnecessary crutch.

Yet why not strive for reaching the highest possible level of leadership? Why not be the best leader you can be? Why not do the best you possibly can at inspiring others? With God involved in your leadership through prayer, you will most definitely be on the high-road-to-leadership track!

Prayer in the Life of a Leader

Of course we would expect that a book about becoming a leader after God's own heart would bring up prayer in the opening chapters. After all, prayer is an essential element of strong leadership.

Why? Because prayer helps make every man a better man—an empowered man. A tuned-into-God leader. A leader after *God's* own heart. Here are a few reasons that prayer is so critical:

- Prayer demonstrates your dependence on God.

- Prayer eliminates pride and self-sufficiency.

- Prayer requires you to look beyond yourself and your own perceived abilities or shortcomings.

- Prayer makes you wait, slows you down. You cannot pray and plow forward at the same time.

- Prayer sharpens your vision. Most decisions are shrouded by the haze of uncertainty, and prayer helps clear away the fog.

- Prayer quiets your heart. You cannot pray and worry at the same time. "Knees don't knock when you kneel on them."[8]

- Prayer energizes faith. Taking time to pray proves you are willing to trust God and spurs you to greater confidence in the Lord and a deeper commitment to His work.

The Power of One Leader's Prayer

You can't read very far in the Bible without meeting up with some of the world's greatest leaders down through time. We see them actively involving God in their personal lives and in the decisions they were making. Like Nehemiah, they knew that only God's intervention could avert disaster. A prime example of this "trust mentality" is found in King Hezekiah (see 2 Kings 18:9—19:37).

In his fourteenth year as king, a massive Assyrian army invaded the now-tiny kingdom of Judah and surrounded Jerusalem. The Assyrian king, Sennacherib, sent a message to Hezekiah mocking the thought of any resistance to Assyria's mighty army. Sennacherib claimed that even the God of the Jews could not protect the people from his might and his powerful army.

So what did Hezekiah, a leader after God's own heart, do? He took the Assyrian king's message and laid it before the altar in the temple in Jerusalem and beseeched God to...

> Open Your eyes, O LORD, and see; and hear the words of Sennacherib, which he has sent to reproach the living God. Truly, LORD, the kings of Assyria have laid waste the nations and their lands, and have cast their gods into the fire...O LORD our God, I pray, save us from his hand, that all the kingdoms of the earth may know that You are the LORD God, You alone (2 Kings 19:16-19).

The result? Hezekiah's prayer was answered. One hundred and eighty-five thousand Assyrian soldiers died in their sleep (verse 35). And the king of Assyria retreated in shame and defeat!

Biblical leaders like Hezekiah owe their greatness to their willingness to pray. Read what E.M. Bounds observed about strong leaders and their prayer life:

> They were not leaders because of brilliance of thought, because they were exhaustless in resources, because of their magnificent culture or native endowment, but because, by the power of prayer, they could command the power of God.[9]

Famous Leaders Who Prayed

When it comes to the leaders in the Bible, you would expect them to be men of prayer, wouldn't you? But many famous leaders not found in the Bible were also men of prayer. I enjoy reading the biographies of great American leaders, and there are two men in particular who prod us to be more faithful in prayer.

One is President Abraham Lincoln. During the darkest hours

of the war between the states, Lincoln often acknowledged his dependence on prayer. In one case, he wrote, "I have been driven many times to my knees by the overwhelming conviction that I had nowhere else to go. My own wisdom and that of those about me seemed insufficient for the day."[10]

The other is Robert E. Lee. Setting politics aside, Lee, the commanding general of the Confederate army during the American Civil War, was not hesitant to exhibit his faith. One story tells of an incident that occurred in December of 1863. General Meade of the Union army came to a place called Mine Run in Virginia, and General Lee's Army of Virginia marched out to meet him. General Lee was riding along his line of battle in the woods when he came upon a party of soldiers holding a prayer meeting on the eve of battle. Lee stopped, dismounted, removed his hat, and stood with an attitude of profound respect and attention while earnest prayer took place. When the prayer gathering was over, General Lee acknowledged each man, got back on his horse, and rode on. All this happened in the midst of the thunder and explosion of the enemy's artillery shells in preparation for the morning's battle.

Long before President Abraham Lincoln and General Robert E. Lee, there was Nehemiah. Who knows—maybe these two nineteenth-century American leaders had learned a lesson or two about prayer from our man of prayer—from Nehemiah. Let's turn our attention back to him as we move onward in our pursuit of becoming leaders after God's own heart.

A Portrait of a Life at Prayer

Nehemiah had just received tragic news: The beloved city of the Jews, Jerusalem, had not been rebuilt. After all these years—90 years!—her walls were still in a state of ruin. And they weren't all that remained in ruins. The people were suffering, oppressed, and humiliated. The report Nehemiah heard was so disturbing that he "sat down and wept, and mourned for many days" (1:4).

How do you usually react when you receive tragic, devastating news—when you're confronted with a serious crisis like that faced by Nehemiah?

It's only natural to react in the way Nehemiah did. When a loved one dies and your heart is broken, even the toughest of guys will usually respond as Nehemiah did. He was emotionally distraught when he received the distressing news about Jerusalem and the condition of the people who had returned from exile. (Who says a leader can't or shouldn't show emotion? Show his heart? Show his feelings?)

But do you let your anguish paralyze you, or do you take the next step as Nehemiah did? "I was fasting and praying before the God of heaven" (verse 4). Do you do as Nehemiah did and start praying before the God of heaven? Do you immediately turn to Him for comfort? To seek His will? To gain a better understanding of what He is allowing to happen in your life? To seek divine direction for making the decisions that must be made?

Nehemiah was a man of great influence in the Persian Empire and before the king. He could have easily taken matters into his own hands. He could have gone on autopilot and handled this matter in the way he had watched his king and employer do time after time. But on this occasion and throughout his story in the Bible, we see a different coping mechanism, a *superior* coping mechanism. We see Nehemiah praying or involved in some aspect of prayer at least 14 times![11]

We don't know what Nehemiah looked like. But we do know that if a portrait of him had been painted and preserved down through the centuries, it just might have shown him bowed in prayer. The book of Nehemiah opens with him praying in response to news about a serious crisis. And oftentimes a portrait isn't painted from a single snapshot. Rather, it's based on many photographs that help the artist to create a composite of a person's life—a composite that includes his personality, passion, purpose, and heart. No, Nehemiah didn't pray only once. His kneeling before God didn't end with the first chapter of the book of Nehemiah. Chapter 1 merely begins to describe his extraordinary life and leadership. And as you read on through his life story, you discover that seeking God's direction through prayer was the constant habit of this remarkable man, this remarkable leader!

The Value of Prayer in the Life of a Leader

As was the case with Nehemiah, your opportunities for prayer never happen in a vacuum. They are usually precipitated by recent events, good or bad. By conversations, letters from missionaries, by hearing of the needs of others. It's important to pray while a burden is burning on your heart. That's what Nehemiah did. When he heard about the problem in Jerusalem, he prayed immediately!

Unfortunately, unless prayer is a natural and regular response to anything and everything big or small, most leaders—including you and me—tend to push back urgent matters of prayer or put them on hold and give priority to lesser things. The opportunity to pray passes while we procrastinate and indulge ourselves in easy or self-serving activities. It seems like there are almost always other "urgent" matters of leadership that snatch away the time we could spend in prayer.

A reality check: To be a leader after God's own heart—even a *man* after God's own heart—you must decide just how important prayer is in your life and the lives of others—those you love, those you lead. Working with God through prayer is a decision that needs to be made and a discipline that has to be developed. Prayer is meaningful, and it is prayer that touches the nerve that moves the hand of God. You must realize that "prayer does not fit us for the greater work, prayer *is* the greater work."

If you expect to be used greatly by God in leadership, you must be a man of prayer.

NEHEMIAH ON LEADERSHIP

As a leader, how can you afford *not* to pray? The burdens of being a good leader are intense, so don't try to shoulder leadership responsibilities alone when you have God available and wanting to help. Remember, you can lead without God, but you can't be a *great* leader without God. Let these principles from Nehemiah's remarkable prayer life guide you to increased strength as you guide others:

- Pray to meet the needs of others. Nehemiah's awareness of the conditions of the people, not just the condition of the city of Jerusalem, moved him to pray and to seek and find a way to help them.

- Pray with an open mind. Be willing to be the answer to your own prayers. As Nehemiah prayed, he caught a vision that God's purpose involved *him*! It is entirely possible that God will reveal His purpose for you as you pray.

- Pray with a willing heart. Nehemiah committed himself to obeying God's leading to use him as a part of the solution. He willingly asked for a leave from his job. You too may have to set aside certain activities so you can carry out God's plan.

- Pray for the vision of others. Nehemiah could not complete God's purpose to build the wall alone, and for most projects, the same will be true for you. Pray for God to put the same burden on the hearts of others so that they too will catch your vision.

- Pray with persistence. Don't give up when it seems God isn't answering you. Persevere no matter what. Nehemiah prayed for four months before he received a clear, concise response from the Lord. And he didn't stop there. Even when faced with a great wall of opposition, he pressed on with prayer until the physical city wall was completed.

- Pray for blameless conduct. Leadership is "as much caught as taught." Pray as Nehemiah did about his own sinfulness and the need for forgiveness. Your strength will increase if you are a clean vessel, fit for the Master's use.

- Pray for direction. Nehemiah prayed at every step along

the journey of doing God's will. He prayed about every step he would take, and then he did something else—he took action.

• Pray and then act. Prayer is not a substitute for action. There should be a balance between prayer and activity, between faith in God and following God, between praying for God's will and doing God's will. Don't put off, in the name of prayer, what you know is right. Sometimes there's only time to lift up an "arrow prayer," and then act. At other times, it's agonizing prayer that could continue for months, as happened in the case of Nehemiah. Or you might not get an answer for years or even decades. But once the answer does come, move out with the strength of faith and watch as God opens doors—or builds a wall!

God's eternal program will not stall without your prayers, but as a leader who prays, others will receive the blessing of your partnership with God for the advancement of His great plan for the ages. To pray or not to pray? It's your choice.

Men may spurn our appeals, reject our message,
oppose our arguments, despise our persons; but
they are helpless against our prayers.[12]

—J. SIDLOW BAXTER

4

COURAGE...SOLIDIFIES YOUR LEADERSHIP

The king said to me,
"Why is your face sad, since you are not sick?
This is nothing but sorrow of heart."
So I became dreadfully afraid

(NEHEMIAH 2:2).

Well, it's time to go to work!

As he did every day, Nehemiah—AKA "The Royal Butler"—poured wine into the king's favorite cup. Like many of the king's prized possessions, it had probably been plundered from a far-off land. The solid-gold chalice was exquisitely shaped and engraved in a foreign nation's script. As Nehemiah poured some of the wine from the cup into his palm, it was now time for Russian roulette Persian style.

At that moment, Nehemiah reflected back upon the elaborate, painstaking care he had taken all day long as he tended to the many meticulous details involved in setting food and drink before the king. Because he was the king's cupbearer, Nehemiah spent countless hours overseeing and inspecting the purchase and preparation of all the king's food. He had accompanied and watched over every servant involved in any part of putting together the king's meal. Throughout the entire preparation process, he never took his eyes off the food and drink. He accompanied the procession of servants as they had laid out the furnishings and the elaborate repast in preparation for the king's arrival to dine.

Yes, now it was time. The food was spread, presented in a manner worthy of the sovereign that King Artaxerxes was. The king and his attendants and guests were seated. It was time for the cupbearer to do his thing. To do his job. It was time for him to taste and test the wine.

Nehemiah carefully and ceremoniously poured out a bit of the fragrant liquid into his left palm. Raising it to his lips, he sipped from it as the king watched. After swallowing the liquid…and after a few crucial minutes passed…and after it became evident that Nehemiah hadn't been affected by or died from the wine…and after Nehemiah had tested the wine for taste, quality, and poison…*and* after he—and all those present—knew the wine he had poured out was fit for a king in every way, Nehemiah handed the golden goblet to his king.

Nehemiah knew that once again, he had done his job successfully. He was good at his job, and he took it seriously. But he also took the troubling news from Jerusalem seriously. He could only hope that his deep concern wouldn't be noticed.

But King Artaxerxes knew his cupbearer well—too well. He knew him almost like a good friend. Something was different about Nehemiah's expression and countenance, and the king noticed. He asked, "Why is your face sad, since you are not sick? This is nothing but sorrow of heart."

Nehemiah's response? He became dreadfully afraid! He hated the anxiety he felt, the apprehension that wound its way around his normally calm heart. Yet fear and all that it threatened was there. Nehemiah knew his life was in danger. He knew this from firsthand observation of the king's erratic behavior. He also knew the next few minutes were crucial. He had to be careful about the words he chose to say or not say.

Courage Is Fear Under Control

It's been said that courage is not the absence of fear. Rather, it's the ability to respond to it in an appropriate manner. You see, fear is not a bad thing. God uses this emotion to insert caution into our actions. Fear in the midst of danger heightens the senses to either fight or flee. It also causes us to use our minds and make quick decisions and reach for solutions. So respect your fear.

Courage, on the other hand, does not dismiss fear. It evaluates the cause for the fear and determines how to proceed. Courage may choose to stand and fight with fear as its companion. Or, in the midst of danger or overwhelming odds, courage will not exchange fear for foolhardiness. It may well choose to retreat in order to fight another day.

Courage Is a Must for a Leader

In his book *The 21 Indispensable Qualities of a Leader*, author John Maxwell places courage at position number 6 out of 21. Under a section entitled "Courage in a Leader Inspires Commitment for Followers," he writes:

> "Courage is contagious," asserts evangelist Billy Graham. "When a brave man takes a stand, the spines of others are stiffened." A show of courage by any person encourages others. But a show of courage by a leader inspires. It makes people want to follow him.[13]

The courage of a leader is revealed in his willingness to face unpleasant—and even devastating!—situations and conditions with composure. Courage acts with firmness in the light of challenge, even though it may mean suffering the consequences of the decision—a decision which will often be unpopular.

Courage in the Lives of Two Leaders

We'll learn more about Martin Luther in the chapter on integrity. But history teaches us that he also possessed the important quality of courage in a remarkable way. It seems that integrity strengthened Luther's courage. Here is one historian's estimation of Luther:

It has been asserted that he was perhaps as fearless a man as ever lived. When he set out on his momentous journey to Worms [the city where he would meet his accusers] he said, "You can expect from me everything save fear of recantation. I shall not flee, much less recant."[14]

Another courageous leader (whom we met earlier) was Robert E. Lee. I can't remember when I first became interested in Civil War history. But to this day, whenever I'm in one of my favorite haunts, a bookstore, I naturally gravitate toward books dealing with the clash between the northern and southern states in nineteenth-century America.

So, as usual, the last time I was in an airport, I made a beeline straight to the bookstore and then straight to the history section. There I found and purchased a biography of the great—though controversial—General Robert E. Lee.

As I began reading the book during the next leg of my flight, I came across an account of Lee's adventures during another war, America's war with Mexico in 1846. Lee's superior officer reported that Lee carried out "the greatest feat of physical and moral courage performed by any individual in my knowledge."[15]

It's no wonder that General Robert E. Lee was such an influential person 15 years later during the Civil War. The same courage Lee showed earlier was evident throughout the war as he led the Army of Virginia and inspired his soldiers to follow, even in the face of overwhelming odds.

Courage in the Midst of Fear

Long before Martin Luther and Robert E. Lee appeared on the scene, there were other leaders whose courage enabled them to know victory and be successful.

Joshua was one such leader. He was a bona fide leader after God's own heart, a worthy study in leadership himself. You can read his story in the Bible, in the book of Joshua. Once you begin reading about him, you will quickly discover Joshua had a bad case of "the fears."

Joshua took over the leadership of Israel immediately after

Moses died. And based on what God says to Joshua, it appears that Joshua was fairly fearful and anxious. But God never rebuked Joshua for this. He only encouraged and exhorted him to be strong and overcome his fears, which were justified because of…

- Joshua's predecessor, Moses. Joshua was expected to follow in the sandals of the bigger-than-life-leader—the same Moses who talked to God and miraculously led the people out of Egypt. Then there was…

- Joshua's army, if you could call it that! His men were a ragtag band with little or no military training and experience in battle. And finally, there was…

- Joshua's enemy who inhabited the land. Joshua had seen them himself. They were giants. They were savage tribes who refused to give up their land without a fierce fight (Numbers 13:32; 14:45).

Being omniscient and knowing all there is to know, God recognized the fear in His rookie general. Repeatedly the Lord comforted and encouraged His new leader. He said to Joshua, "Be strong and of good courage…for the LORD your God is with you wherever you go" (Joshua 1:9)

Now, think about this. God's powerful promise given to His hesitant leader, Joshua, was also available to Nehemiah hundreds of years later. And, good news! It is amazingly still available to you today, more than 2400 years later.

Whether you are currently an active leader or just now being exposed to the concept, you can draw on the following three reasons why you can always act with courage. These three reasons tell you why you never need to let fear immobilize you, why you can be courageous in fighting the battles you face as a man and as a leader.

1. Courage Grows from God's Character

God said to Joshua, "Be strong and of good courage" (Joshua 1:9).

He was like a coach—the *ultimate* coach—on the sidelines, encouraging Joshua to, in essence, lead these people to victory—give them the land!

"Why, Lord?" we might wonder along with Joshua.

"Because I swore to their fathers to give them possession of the land," the Lord explained (see Joshua 1:6).

End of discussion! God promised it…and it was as good as done.

This meant Joshua could go into battle with courage, knowing that God, who cannot lie, had promised victory. God was not going to allow His servant Joshua to fail nor flail on fulfilling His promise to the people.

God's reassurance of His promise to Joshua should give you, as a leader in your sphere of influence, this same confidence. God has promised you the victory. You must believe this. You must trust God. "Thanks be to God, who *always* leads us in His triumph in Christ" (2 Corinthians 2:14). Your triumph in Him is a given. Your promised victory should give you courage and confidence in the battles you face and fight in everyday life.

2. Courage Expands with God's Guidance

Maybe Joshua was still wavering. Maybe he wasn't quite sure he wanted the job of leader. (And maybe you can relate!) Whatever Joshua was thinking, God told him again, for the second time, "Be strong and very courageous" (Joshua 1:7). In essence, God coached his tentative handpicked leader, "Take even *more* courage, Joshua!"

Why, Lord?

"Because I have given you the battle plans that will guide you to success! And now I'm giving you all the strength you will need to pull it off, to make it happen."

God gave Joshua guidance, and He gives it to you, too, through His Word. So, as God cautioned Joshua, "do according to all the law which Moses My servant commanded you" (verse 7).

This reminds me of a story I heard of a championship football team that was defeated by a weaker team. It didn't matter what play was run—the opponent seemed to know exactly how to defend against the play. The coaches on the stronger team were baffled as they tried to make sense of their loss. Then, sometime later, the mystery was solved: The opposing team had somehow obtained one of their team's playbooks. The stolen playbook gave the opposing team a guide to victory. They knew every play the other team might possibly attempt.

God has given you a playbook as well—the Bible. This means you can make a strong, successful defense against fear and the flaming missiles of the evil one (Ephesians 6:16). So purpose to follow God's advice to Joshua. Don't get distracted and lose your courage. Don't turn to the right or to the left. Keep your devotion focused on God and His playbook for your life. "Then you will have good success...wherever you go" (Joshua 1:8-9).

3. Courage Multiplies with God's Presence

Log this well: God promised to be with Joshua *wherever* he went. For the third time, God told His leader, "Be strong and courageous." And then the Lord added, "Do not be afraid, nor be dismayed." Why? "For the LORD your God is with you wherever you go" (Joshua 1:9).

I'm sure that in the past, you've faced difficult situations or illnesses. Or you've had demanding meetings or rigorous commitments you had to brave. Or you've played in a big game or match or had to perform in a major production or give an important speech or faced the pressure of teaching a difficult lesson at church or Bible study. Everyone's been there, in a place where they really needed to be brave and do well.

And I'm sure you also know how encouraging it is when you have family and friends or a mentor nearby to support and cheer you on. Their presence and care provide a stimulus for you to do your best. It gives you the courage to do the right thing.

Well, it's even more motivating to know that God is always nearby—right there with you—no matter what happens and no matter where you go. This was Joshua's secret to his courage. And it should be yours, too, as you make your way through every challenge.

A Profile of Courage

Now back to our hero, to Nehemiah. He didn't have the personal reassurance from God that was given to Joshua: God did not tell Nehemiah three times not to be afraid, but to be filled with courage instead. But Nehemiah did have knowledge of God's track record of faithfulness to rely on. His response to his fear at the moment his emotions were exposed was a pivotal point in his life and in God's use of him. If Nehemiah caved in to fear, if he pleaded for his life, if he begged for forgiveness, the story of his remarkable feat and brilliant leadership and positive contribution to God's purposes would have come to an end. Yes, giving in to fear and cowardice was definitely one option—and the easy option!

But no. Nehemiah chose to focus his heart, soul, mind, and strength on trusting God. And, as the saying goes, the rest is history. His choice to face his fears with the strength of the Lord was the springboard for an amazing life of leadership and success. Rather than succumb to the fear of what King Artexerxes might do or the possibility of facing the end of his life, Nehemiah determined to be courageous. And that opened the door to a limitless future—a future God had in mind for Nehemiah and for the betterment of His people.

The book of Nehemiah gives us a description of what courage looks like:

Courage starts in the heart—Courage is not an instantaneous emotion or automatic response. The outward signs of courage result from the hard-fought battles of a reasoning heart and a questioning mind. It fights against putting the needs of self before the needs of others. In Nehemiah's case, it was a struggle to seek and participate in the solution to restore the city of God's people. The rise of courage for Nehemiah started with prayer, with a praying heart. Where is your present battlefield? Be sure you pray.

Courage takes risks—Taking risks appears to be a common denominator of highly effective leaders. They are risk-takers. Nehemiah's responsible position as cupbearer to the king came because he took risks every time he tasted the king's food or tested his wine. He was a courageous man. His courage each time he tested the king's drink was based on his trust in his own skills and diligence.

Once Nehemiah's sadness was noticed and exposed by the king, his courage enabled him to take the necessary risks. Drawing on the strength and courage of the Lord, he boldly explained his grief, asked permission to leave, and sought the king's help. Nothing in his requests could be brought about from his own abilities. The answers to his requests had to come from someone else—the king.

And so Nehemiah appealed to King Artexerxes, completely trusting in the sovereign hand of God to move the king's heart. As Solomon wrote, "the king's heart is in the hand of the LORD, like the rivers of water; He turns it wherever He wishes" (Proverbs 21:1). Are you in a tough spot? Trust in the Lord and face it head-on.

Courage attempts the impossible—It doesn't take any amount of courage to do the ordinary. Doing the routine is simply doing your duty. But attempting the impossible takes audacity—chutzpa. What Nehemiah was considering to undertake was the impossible. After all, others had failed for at least 90 years to rebuild the walls around Jerusalem and reestablish the city of God that lay in rubble and dust. Yet it was this very undertaking that Nehemiah asked for, received permission and supplies for, and struck out across a barren land to Judea. That's a bodacious request—that's courage! Remember Nehemiah's courage the next time you are tempted to think that doing God's will is impossible.

Courage takes a stand—Intimidation is the favorite tool of the bully, and the nations surrounding Jerusalem were bullies. They threatened military force in order to keep the Jews—God's people, the apple of His eye—suppressed and afraid. Even though greatly outnumbered, Nehemiah, once he arrived in Jerusalem, took a stand

against his adversaries. He stepped up to defend the workers on the
wall as they labored to rebuild it. Nehemiah's courageous act, actually a bluff, brought unexpected positive results—the bullies bought
it and backed off! Ask God for greater courage when you need to
speak up and take a stand.

Courage seeks justice—Courage is not pugnacious. It doesn't look for
a fight. In fact, courage understands that more strength is needed
to *not* fight. But grave injustices had been done against the poor of
Judea. Therefore Nehemiah sought justice. Courage will fight for
the welfare of the needy, and Nehemiah possessed the quality of
courage to make a stand and fight the good fight. As a leader, he was
willing to take on the rich ruling class in order for justice to prevail.
As a leader, always keep your eyes, ears—and heart—open for news
of injustice. Then do all you can to make things right.

Courage does the right thing—Courage makes the difficult choices,
and right choices are usually difficult. And fear can cloud a leader's
mind and judgment. Nehemiah was warned by seemingly author-
itative people-in-the-know that he should flee from his project in
Jerusalem and hide from his enemies. But Nehemiah chose not
to take the advice. Instead, he stood firm and was willing to fight.
Courage does the right thing even with the possibility of its own
demise. A strong prayer life will guide your choices as you seek to
do the right thing.

Courage is not selfish—It takes a special leader to share the "lime-
light of success." Over half of Nehemiah's story in the Bible shows
him to be the unquestioned leader. Nehemiah saved the day. He
defended the city. He motivated others to build the wall. Yet at the
height of his popularity, he stepped aside and allowed Ezra, a man
more qualified, to lead the people in worship. Ask God to make you
keenly aware when your part is done or maxed out and it's time to
step aside.

Courage does not compromise—Nor does courage go out of date.

Nehemiah spent 12 years defending the city of Jerusalem, its people, and especially God and His Word. His decisions were often unpopular and hotly contested by his Jewish brethren and the surrounding hostile nations.

Nehemiah then returned to Susa for a time. Later he traveled back to Jerusalem, where he once again faced many of the same issues, and some that were worse than before. Nehemiah courageously picked up where he had left off. He remained uncompromising in his leadership of the Jews against injustice and worldly conformity. You will often have to take the heat for leading toward what is right. Don't ever slow down! Keep on keeping on.

NEHEMIAH ON LEADERSHIP

Whoever you are leading, they expect you, as their leader, to be courageous. To be calm under fire. To not falter when facing difficult and unpleasant situations. Your followers draw their strength and courage—and example—from you. Nehemiah was a success because he was willing to take risks and trust God with the results.

You can be this kind of a leader too. The real question is, are you up for the task? And another question is, what can you do to continue growing as a leader? This requires work every day and in every way: Look to God. Trade in your fears for His courage. Draw upon the strength He extends to you all day long.

Nehemiah's life is a testament to courage. God is looking for leaders like Nehemiah to fight moral, physical, political, and spiritual battles. He is looking for those who possess the spiritual courage to trust Him and take their faith in Him into the daily battles of life. He is looking for leaders—like you—who possess the courage...

- to stand up for Christ in public, at work, and at home
- to model godly character to others
- to guide their family out of worldliness and into godliness
- to live a consistent life for Christ, regardless of the cost

Whenever you feel like your courage is weak or faltering, realize there is no shame in that. The proven leaders and giants of the faith—like Nehemiah and Joshua—faltered, but they did not fall. Follow these few steps to strengthen and improve a courage in you that may falter, but will never fall.

1. Draw strength, power, and resolve from God's character, God's Word, and God's presence (Joshua 1:8-9).

2. Determine your ideals. Know what you believe and why. Courage comes once you are willing to fight for those ideals.

3. Test your courage. Don't be afraid to stretch yourself. Courage comes as you overcome hurdles, which makes you stronger for the next test of courage.

4. Remember that God is with you. He's there—always—to help you lead and fight your battles wherever they are fought. Be strong and courageous!

Since God is with you and you are with God, you have nothing to fear!

5

WISDOM...PROMOTES YOUR LEADERSHIP

*"If it pleases the king, and if your servant
has found favor in your sight,
I ask that you send me to Judah"...
So it pleased the king to send me*

(NEHEMIAH 2:5-6).

It was truly a moment of heart-stopping suspense. Up until this very minute, Nehemiah had been the perfect picture of cool, assured composure. It hadn't been easy to appear calm since he had heard from his brother about the shameful and frightening condition of the city of Jerusalem and its people. But Nehemiah found personal solace and public strength by privately praying and planning.

For more than three months it seemed like he had prayed non-stop. He focused every prayer of his heart and every thought and used every spare minute wrestling in prayer for a solution to the predicament God's people were in. He focused on patiently and meticulously preparing for the right opportunity to speak to the king about his concern.

Up until this very second, there had been more than a three-month interval between that fateful day when Nehemiah had received the distressing news and now, this awkward moment with the king. It was time to put courage to work. He had rehearsed his speech a thousand times and felt he was ready. (Well, at least *mentally* he had played this moment over and over!)

For the same three months he had wondered exactly *when* the moment would arrive that he would have to speak up before the king. He had played through several possible scenarios in his mind. *Maybe it would come at a time when he sensed the king was in a good mood. Or maybe the right moment would present itself when there would be very few people in the king's presence. Or maybe the perfect time would become obvious some evening after dinner, when the king was relaxed, filled, and content.*

But as it turned out, it was none of the above. The king's mood and the setting had nothing to do with it. When it happened, the king was surrounded by guests at his table—including the queen! And never mind a few private words after a relaxing dinner. Dinner was still being served when Nehemiah's chance arrived. Instead, out of the blue, the king saw sadness on Nehemiah's face. And out of concern, he asked, "Why is your face sad, since you are not sick?"

Nehemiah gulped and recognized the opportunity God had orchestrated—a divine opportunity Nehemiah could never have dreamed up! *Praise God*, Nehemiah celebrated in his heart. *The king is actually concerned, and he is asking me for a reason for my sadness!* Then, as Nehemiah opened his mouth, he prayed to the God of heaven and asked, Lord, *give me wisdom! Here goes!*

Wisdom Doesn't Just Happen!

It's true: Wisdom doesn't just happen. It takes time and effort to gather, process, and incorporate wisdom and put it to use. Take, for instance, man's first flight. That's what happened on December 17, 1903. On a cold and windy beach, five people and a dog watched history being made. The place was Kitty Hawk, North Carolina. The event was the first time that a heavier-than-air object had lifted off from the ground on its own power and sustained a controlled flight. This major milestone in history lasted only a few brief seconds, but the age of flight had begun! Orville Wright, age 32, piloted the Flyer, as it was named, 10 feet off the ground for about 120 feet.

Later that same day, Wilbur, Orville's older brother, flew their plane a distance of 800 feet. The accomplishments of these two men represent a life of incurable optimism and dauntless labor and study. For years they had researched the efforts of others who had tried and failed. They had built and tested endless models before designing and building the Flyer.

The wisdom needed to make this happen was the end result of long years of trial and error. But when it comes to daily living, wouldn't it be faster—and certainly less painful!—to bypass the trials and errors and just do things right the first time? To get wisdom without the hit-and-miss efforts? To gain it from the start?

Well, fellow leader, that's exactly what God wants to do for you. He promises wisdom. He promises that if you *ask* for wisdom, you will have it. Now, *that* is a powerful promise! Read it for yourself:

> If any of you lacks wisdom, let him ask of God, who gives to all liberally and without reproach, and it will be given to him (James 1:5).

Understanding Wisdom

We'll examine Nehemiah's exploits in a few pages and see first-hand how wisdom exhibited itself throughout his biography. For now, let's dig into an understanding of the heart and soul of wisdom.

Wisdom Has Its Source in God

Everything has a source. It starts somewhere, as my family discovered during one summer vacation in Montana. While on the road, we drove over a short bridge with a sign that read, "Missouri River." Earlier we had been to St. Louis and seen the impressive width of the Missouri River just before it empties into the mighty Mississippi. Well, by contrast, this part of the Missouri River, way up in Montana, was small—only a little more than a creek. So I backed up the car to make certain we hadn't misread the sign. Sure enough, we were looking at the beginnings of the Missouri River. We weren't far from its source.

Here's something to ponder: Everything has a source…except God. God is the source of all things. Chances are you already know that the heavens and earth have their source in God (Genesis 1:1). But did you know that wisdom has its source in God too? God *is* wisdom (Ezra 7:25). And His wisdom and knowledge are derived from no one (Job 21:22). All true wisdom is found in Him alone. So as a leader of a family, your peers, or a corporation who needs wisdom for the task, look to God and His Word.

Wisdom Is More than Knowledge

You've probably met some leaders who, when you first met them, really impressed you. But in time, as you got to know them better and witnessed a little more of their leadership up close, you began to realize there wasn't much connection between their knowledge and their leadership. Their ability to lead was less than successful. Why? They lacked wisdom.

By contrast, there are many leaders who are uneducated and possess little or no formal training, yet they are wise in the decisions they make.

You don't need a formal education to make use of the wisdom presented in God's Word. This wisdom is what enables a person to think clearly and make the best decisions—even in the midst of difficult situations and emergencies.

Like most people, you probably think that you could use more of this kind of wisdom. Well, the good news is that God freely offers this kind of wisdom to you. Read on!

Wisdom Is Available

Are you experiencing any problems or trials in your life or in your role as a leader? Are you at a crossroad in your career? Could you use some direction in dealing with a family member or a friend or workmate? Are you struggling through some difficult issues? Or are you perhaps needing some help in the all-of-the-above category? Then you need wisdom—God's wisdom.

Have you already asked God for help? God has promised you wisdom. He calls out, "If any of you lacks wisdom, let him ask of God" (James 1:5). My friend, whatever issue or problem you are facing, you don't have to argue, debate, express your views and thoughts for days or weeks on end. You don't have to agonize or grope around in the dark, hoping to stumble upon answers through trial and error. Whenever you need wisdom, you can pray to God—you can "ask of God"...and wisdom "will be given" to you (verse 5)!

Wisdom Is Freely Given

Have you ever had to ask for a loan? The loan officer probably took a lot of time with your application. He may have exercised such great caution you began to think it was his own money he was lending you! Having to make such a request can be agony. If you're at all like me, you probably walked out of that bank hoping you would never have to go through that experience again.

God's response to your requests for wisdom is just the opposite. He "gives to all liberally" (James 1:5). God doesn't just dole out wisdom a little here and a little there. And He doesn't make you wait in line to receive it. And He doesn't give it grudgingly. No, He gives "to all" who ask. He gives His wisdom freely, liberally, generously, and with an open hand.

God also doesn't dole out a lecture every time you come to Him asking, "May I have some more wisdom, please?" No, each time you ask, wisdom is given "without reproach." With this kind of promise, and this kind of freedom, why oh why aren't we beating a path to God on a regular basis?

Wisdom Comes in a Variety of Ways

While the Missouri River has one source, it also has many tributaries along its path that add to its size and power as it flows toward its destiny, the Mississippi. What "wisdom tributaries" does God feed into your life to strengthen and mature you, to make you wise?

- *Your walk with God*—Wisdom comes as you develop a God-awareness, as you walk with and follow Him, as you grow a more conscious, worshipful attitude toward Him. The foundation of wisdom is to fear the Lord (Proverbs 1:7). As you honor and esteem God, live in awe of His power, and obey His Word, His wisdom becomes your wisdom. It's yours as you allow Him to become the controlling influence in your life.

  A pearl of wisdom for you: Going to church and worshiping God helps start your week with the right focus and a dose of His wisdom.

- *Your time in God's Word*—God's Word can make you wise—wiser than your enemies, your teachers, even those older and more experienced than you. How can you get this wisdom? It's simple. All you have to do is love God's Word, hold it first in your heart and mind, and obey it (Psalm 119:98-100).

  A pearl of wisdom for you: Digging into God's Word daily will get the Bible into you. And reading good Christian books and devotionals that are solidly based on Scripture will help too.

- *Your input from others*—You can gain wisdom through seeking the advice of those who possess wisdom. Find them. Watch their lives. Seek them out. Ask them questions. You can also read the wise and godly advice of others through Christian books. In seeking the wisdom of others, you grow in maturity as a leader.

  A pearl of wisdom for you: Pray and ask God for mentors. Ask Him to show you who might be available to help you. Ask that person if the two of you can get together and talk. And pay a visit to your Christian bookstore. See what books are available that can help you advance in wisdom.

Nehemiah's Life of Wisdom

We've already determined that Nehemiah had to have been a pretty smart guy. And, beyond the grace of God, he had to have been extremely wise in his actions around an employer who was, according to historians, emotionally unstable. As you read his story in the Bible, you see specific clues as to what wisdom looks like in the life of Nehemiah. Here are a few signs you can't miss:

Nehemiah sought answers—Here is a life lesson in leadership from Nehemiah: "I asked them concerning the Jews...and concerning Jerusalem" (1:2). A leader needs information—facts—in order to make wise decisions. He wasn't about to act without knowing the facts. No wise leader—of a family or a Fortune 500 company and everything in between—moves into action without being armed with information.

Nehemiah sought advice—When a problem showed up on Nehemiah's doorstep, his first response was to seek God's advice: "When I heard these words [regarding the dire condition in Jerusalem]...I sat down and wept, and mourned for many days; I was fasting and praying before the God of heaven" (1:4). Nehemiah knew he needed God's strength, God's help, and God's wisdom. So he prayed "before the God of heaven." When you encounter trouble, pray! Pray Paul's prayer: "Lord, what do You want me to do?" (Acts 9:6).

Nehemiah was patient—"It came to pass in the month of Nisan...I took the wine and gave it to the king" (Nehemiah 2:1). We already know that Nehemiah prayed and fasted and planned for more than three months before he acted. Wisdom is never in a hurry. Try not to make hasty decisions. Take time to think, pray, and seek advice. Paraphrasing General George S. Patton's leadership advice, "Take as long as you can to make a decision, but do make a decision."

Nehemiah was prudent—Even a "fearless leader" experiences fear. Nehemiah testified, "I became dreadfully afraid" (2:2). How does a leader overcome fear? Through wisdom. Wisdom is careful. It doesn't take anything for granted. Nehemiah enjoyed great privilege, but he knew his king's disposition. His caution, prudence, and constant prayer ensured that he spoke his concerns and request in a respectful manner. He used past experience to teach him caution. As the prudent shoe salesman learned to say, "Madam, this shoe is too small for your foot," not "Madam, your foot is too big for this shoe."

Nehemiah was prepared—Following all of wisdom's steps, Nehemiah made his request of the king: "I ask that you send me to Judah" (2:5). He had already prayed and planned. Then, when the right time arrived, he acted wisely. A wise leader prays and plans, and never joins a meeting without knowing what he's going to say. Such a leader even prepares for the questions, concerns, and objections others may have to his plan. In other words, his "ducks are all lined up."

Nehemiah sought justice—We'll see this illustrated in more detail later in this book. We will learn that some of God's people were being seriously mistreated. The privileged class was unjustly charging interest on loans to the people, something expressly forbidden in God's law. What did wisdom do? What did *Nehemiah* do? "After serious thought, I rebuked the nobles and rulers, and said to them, 'Each of you is exacting usury from his brother'" (5:7). Notice again that wisdom gathers the facts first, *then* takes its time to carefully determine the right actions.

Nehemiah sought solutions—Wisdom guided Nehemiah to successfully rebuild the city wall. But what to do about repopulating the city was his next problem. Once again, because of his walk with God, Nehemiah could say, "My God put it into my heart to" register the people by genealogy (7:5). Then lots (something like dice) were cast, and one out of ten families was asked to move into the city (11:1). Wisdom's solution was to let the "lot" choose those who must uproot their families and move into the city.

NEHEMIAH ON LEADERSHIP

Every Christian leader—in fact, every *Christian*—should want to be a person of wisdom. Not once are the words *wise* or *wisdom* used in the Bible with regard to Nehemiah's life. Yet time after time he is seen making sensible decisions. What was the secret behind his stunning success?

We already know Nehemiah was familiar with the Scriptures. And we know he was obedient to them. His "fear of the LORD" was the beginning of his wisdom, just as Proverbs 9:10 says. How about you? What steps can you take to become a leader marked by wisdom—a leader after God's own heart?

Crave wisdom—Want it above all else! King Solomon shows us what this focused heart-attitude looks like. God gave him a chance to request anything he wanted: "Ask! What shall I give you?" How did Solomon reply? (And what would you have said?) Solomon asked God for wisdom—for "an understanding heart" (1 Kings 3:5,9).

Wisdom is the above-all, end-all best trait to desire. As Solomon teaches, forget riches. Forget fame. "Happy is the man who finds wisdom, and the man who gains understanding. For her proceeds are better than the profits of silver, and her gain than fine gold" (Proverbs 3:13-14).

> *Some questions for your heart:* How do the desires of your heart measure up? Do you wish for riches? For a long life? For power? For name recognition? Or do you wish for wisdom? Are you seeking the world's answers to true happiness or God's answers? Set your heart—and sights—on seeking and craving God's wisdom.

Plead for wisdom—God promises wisdom if you "ask of God" for it (James 1:5). How do you "ask of God"? Through prayer. Prayer acknowledges your dependence on Him. And because your wisdom is in short supply and is short-term, you need to be constantly asking God—constantly praying—for His wisdom to manage your life and the leading of others.

Some questions for your heart: Most guys have plenty of time to read the sports and financial sections of the newspaper, or to busy themselves with all kinds of quests online. But somehow prayer doesn't get worked into their busy schedule. Is prayer slotted into your appointment book? Is it on your daily to-do list? Is it a part of each day's routine? God isn't calling you to break any records for the longest prayer session. But He *is* calling you to pray. And you should call upon Him for wisdom daily. Ask for it. Plead for it! Pray "Lord, give me wisdom."

Seek wisdom—Wisdom is promised…but *you* must seek it. Wisdom calls…but *you* must answer. To discover the treasure of wisdom, you need to follow God's treasure map: "The Lord gives wisdom." But where does it come from? Where can this treasure be found? "From His mouth come knowledge and understanding" (Proverbs 2:6). Dig into God's Word, and *you* will become rich in wisdom!

Some questions for your heart: How's your Bible-reading time these days? Is it nonexistent? Are you doing better? Is there room for improvement? God's wisdom is in His Word. And He says you are to actively "seek [wisdom] as silver, and search for her as for hidden treasures" (Proverbs 2:4).

Nurture wisdom—Wisdom has to be fed, cultivated, and tended to regularly. It's not permanent. Nor does it perpetuate itself. It must be sought day after day…every day…for a lifetime. And once you obtain God's treasure of sound wisdom, it is for today—and today only. Use it with God's blessings as you lead those you love and guide. Use it to make good, better, and best choices. But don't count on today's wisdom for tomorrow's needs. Tomorrow, get up and seek fresh wisdom. Your life is constantly changing, so your need to work at wisdom on a daily basis is paramount. To continue being a person marked and led by wisdom, you need to nurture wisdom continually.

Some questions for you: Commitment is key. At what level would you rate your commitment to growing in daily wisdom? High?

Mediocre? Seriously low? Do you have a plan? It only takes about two minutes to read one chapter of Proverbs—God's Book of Wisdom. Try reading one chapter of Proverbs a day for a month (read Proverbs 1 on the first day of the month, Proverbs 2 on the second day, and so on). Then commit to doing this for life. Soon you will possess the world's greatest treasure—wisdom, a gold mine of resources for strengthening your leadership.

> *Wisdom...is that quality that enables one to*
> *live a noticeably, recognizably outstanding life.*
> *Imagine how much this wonderful thing called*
> *wisdom can contribute to effective leadership.*[16]

6

PLANNING...BRINGS FOCUS TO YOUR LEADERSHIP

Then the king said to me, "What do you request?"
So I prayed to the God of heaven. And I said to the king...
"I ask that you send me to Judah, to the city
of my fathers' tombs, that I may rebuild it"

(NEHEMIAH 2:4-5).

T he feelings that stir within a person's heart when he realizes God is in the process of answering his prayers is hard to explain. So you can imagine Nehemiah probably felt a mixture of excitement, joy, and hesitation when King Artexerxes asked him, "What do you request?" Right that moment he uttered a quick prayer before speaking to the king. The past few months had been agonizingly difficult for Nehemiah, and unexpectedly, God had given him a chance to make his concerns known to the king. But what should he say? He was probably thinking fast on his feet: *If I was planning a 1000-mile desert expedition, let's see...I would need this many camels, this much food. Oh, and I'd need to make sure I knew the locations of the different oases where we could find plenty of water.*

These were likely the sorts of thoughts and plans that now flashed across Nehemiah's mind. From the time he had heard about the sad condition of Jerusalem and its walls, he had probably been planning, day by day, what he would need if he were to make an expedition to Jerusalem. Ideas had constantly popped into his head each day as he prayed. Yes, for months Nehemiah had prayed like he had never prayed before. He had prayed for his beleaguered nation and people. But he had also prayed over the practical issues that came with formulating a plan. And he had prayed that he would keep his mind and heart open to however God might work to make things right in Jerusalem.

And never mind there were still many issues that he and other Jews were facing right there in Susa!

Yet as Nehemiah, a leader after God's own heart, continued to pray day after day, he couldn't get the need for a plan out of his mind. So at some point, after days of repeated battle between praying and thinking, Nehemiah decided to put together a plan. He feverishly began figuring out the quantities of supplies that were necessary, the authorizations that would be needed to rebuild the wall and city, and more. And after he determined these things, he lifted the needs up to God in prayer. He looked out a window that faced toward Jerusalem and prayed, "God, to make this happen, a person would need this many camels, this much food, and…"

Two Types of People

Let's pause for a moment here and consider this: There are two types of people in the world when it comes to planning:

The Type 1 Person—These people don't plan. Oh, they may *think* they have plans. But in reality what they have are dreams, and few if any plans! They merely drift through life, bouncing from pillar to post, like a ball in an old-fashioned pinball machine. Normally those who don't plan don't prosper: "The plans of the diligent *lead* surely to plenty" (Proverbs 21:5). There's a long-time adage that says, "Planning ahead will get you ahead."

If you are a Type 1 person who doesn't plan, maybe now is the time to start. It's as simple as making a list of things you need to do today, tomorrow, next week, and next year. If you don't plan your day, you can be sure someone else will plan it for you. So be the master of your day by planning—and mastering your plan—for your every day.

The Type 2 Person—These people plan ahead. Planning is a life-style and a discipline for these managers and leaders. They have lists, schedules, and goals. And they are producing results. Wherever they place their focus and attention, things happen. Things get done.

This is the good news! But the bad news is that sometimes when these people make their plans, they focus only on the physical and neglect those things that are spiritual and of eternal and personal value—things like a closer relationship with God and family. If you are a Type 2 person—a person who plans—evaluate your focus. Make sure that you include in your plans time for God and your family. These are the priorities that really matter.

To Plan or Not to Plan—That Is the Question

Where were you on June 6, 1944? Or were you even born on or before this momentous day in history? For decades, historians have tried to explain the events that occurred on the day referred to as D-Day, or Decision Day or Disembarkation Day.

On that day, 160,000 Allied troops landed on the shores of Normandy, France. This invasion involved 5000 ships carrying men and vehicles across the English Channel, as well as 800 planes dropping over 13,000 men by parachute. An additional 300 planes released bombs on German troops who were defending the French beaches. The invasion, also called Operation Overlord, involved five massive stages of landings by American, British, and Canadian troops.

Within one year of this successful but costly operation, the fanatical leader of Nazi Germany, Adolf Hitler, committed suicide, and the war in Europe was over.

Obviously, the success of this day didn't "just happen." How did it become reality? One word—*planning*. American General Dwight D. Eisenhower and his staff had spent countless days, weeks, and months planning this massive one-day undertaking. It still stands today as the largest amphibious invasion ever to take place in history.

Planning as a Part of Leadership

So, how seriously do you take the discipline of planning ahead?

Undoubtedly, D-Day would not have succeeded if Eisenhower and his aides hadn't taken the time to plan and coordinate the thousands of details involved in the operation. They were prepared.

And then there was Nehemiah. He wasn't a military general planning a massive invasion. But he was every bit the leader as he planned his own monumental undertaking. He tackled and took on the planning of something no one had been able to accomplish in more than 90 years.

If you are looking for a simple definition for the activity of planning, open just about any dictionary. Here's a composite of what most would say: Planning is to work out, in advance, a method of doing something.

Sounds pretty simple, doesn't it? Here's how one leader described planning: "Planning is an attempt to move from 'now' to 'then,' to change things from 'the way things are' to 'the way things ought to be.'"[17]

Unfortunately, many people don't take planning seriously, including those who are in leadership positions. They have a great idea, and they're so eager to make things happen they don't take time to plan ahead! Or they have a deadline and, in their hurry to complete a project on time, they don't take time to plan and ensure the task gets done well.

In short, they don't understand how important planning is to successful leadership. Here's how time manager Edwin Bliss views the importance of planning:

> There is no more productive use of time than planning ahead. Studies prove what common sense tells us: the more time we spend in advance planning on a project, the less total time is required for it. Don't let today's busy work crowd planning time out of your schedule.[18]

Setting the Scene

Nehemiah was a man of prayer. And it was *as* he prayed that he began to realize his personal responsibility. While it was God's responsibility to lead Nehemiah and answer his prayers, it was Nehemiah's responsibility to plan ahead and be ready.

As we learned earlier, Nehemiah first received the news about the condition of Jerusalem in the month of *Chislev* (November-December). As we come to the encounter between King Artexerxes and Nehemiah, about four months have passed. We're in the month of *Nisan* (March-April).

During all that time, Nehemiah had successfully hidden his emotions and concern regarding the condition of the Jews and the city of Jerusalem. But on this day, the king noticed something different in Nehemiah's behavior. He perceived that Nehemiah was sad. This provoked the king's curiosity, and he asked, "Why is your face sad, since you are not sick? This is nothing but sorrow of heart" (2:2).

Nehemiah was instantly fearful. A servant was never to allow negative emotions to show in the king's presence because it might, in some way, suggest dissatisfaction with the king. To do so could jeopardize a servant's position…or even his life. At the same time, Nehemiah had spent the last four months praying and planning. He knew that eventually he would have to ask the king for help. His request would be a bold one—so bold that he would be risking his life! But because he had been praying for months about this opportunity and planned ahead, he was ready when the king asked his question.

Qualities of an Effective Planner

When Artaxerxes asked Nehemiah why he was sad, Nehemiah realized this was his break, his big opportunity! And he was ready to make his request of the king. He had not only been praying; he had also been burning the midnight oil making detailed plans. Now, fully prepared by months of praying and planning, in a split second, Nehemiah offered up a quick prayer to God, then proceeded to lay out his plan before the king. The way in which he did all this reveals these qualities about a planner:

Passion—An effective planner must have passion. If you don't feel strongly about what you are proposing, how can you expect others to get excited as well? Nehemiah was willing to pay the price to attempt—and hopefully complete—the rebuilding of Jerusalem. He was willing to, at the very least, forfeit his very influential job, and possibly even his life.

How passionate are you? What ideas drive you to your knees in prayer to God? What projects keep you up at night because you are so excited about the future? What incites passion in your heart? Would you say it's your family? Your ministry to others? Your commitment to your work? Your service to your country or community? Pray for passion…and plan with passion.

Support—An effective planner must have support. To make an idea or a plan become reality, a leader needs and secures others with experience, influence, and resources to help make it happen. Nehemiah knew this project he was about to discuss with the king required more clout and funding and provisions than he or even all of the most influential Jews in his local community possessed. So Nehemiah needed to go as far up the "food chain" as possible to ask for the kind of help that would make it possible to fulfill the plans on his mind and heart. And the king was the one at the very top. No one was more powerful than this sovereign. No one had more resources than this man. Nehemiah went to the one person in the kingdom who could help him.

But there was one big problem: The king was unpredictable! And he had been flooded with reports that opposed all thoughts of restoring the ruins in and around Jerusalem. How would he respond to Nehemiah's request?

There is a time to pray. There is a time to plan. And then there is a time to act—and ask. What stage are you in as you follow God's leading? If it's time to pray, pray. If it's time to plan, plan. And if it's time to ask, ask. Who do you know that can help you carry out God's purposes? Identify those people, pray again…and then ask for support.

A clear-cut objective—An effective planner must have a clear-cut objective. There must be a goal in mind that is easily understood, without too many variables, and has a desirable outcome. Otherwise, no one will be able to support the project and lend the much-needed help. Nehemiah's request to the king was simple: "Send me to Judah, to the city of my fathers' tombs, that I may rebuild it" (2:5).

And here's another lesson to the wise: In the simplicity of a request that stated his clear-cut objective, Nehemiah did not mention the name *Jerusalem*—perhaps to keep from touching a political nerve with the king.

A time frame—An effective planner has a time frame in mind. Any plan that doesn't have a proposed beginning and ending date will usually fail. People need a vision for what the project looks like and how long it will take to complete it. They want to know what they are committing themselves to, what's involved. This is exactly what the king and queen asked Nehemiah. "How long will your journey be? And when will you return?" Nehemiah's response? "I set him a time" (verse 6).

What was the time frame of Nehemiah's mission? Only later do we find out that the project lasted 12 years (5:14). It's not clear if this was the time Nehemiah gave to the king, or if delays extended the original request. Regardless of how it played out, there is no indication that the king was upset with the amount of time Nehemiah requested.

Because Nehemiah was an effective leader, he planned. And because he was an effective planner, he had a specific time frame for his plan. As a leader, remember to always make your plans with a calendar in hand.

Permission—An effective planner seeks permission. Every plan needs approval from someone. Let's say you want to build a house or an office building. You've already received approval for a loan. And you have your set of floor plans. And you've even purchased the land. But you still need one key thing before you can make your plan work, make your dream come true, make it become reality. You need permission and approval from the zoning commission.

Nehemiah knew he needed some serious permission. A part of his meticulous planning made it clear that the three months of travel from Susa to Jerusalem would be dangerous. He couldn't just go wherever he wanted. He needed to follow political protocol and get letters of introduction from King Artexerxes—letters that would be required for passage from one province to another.

Yes, he needed some major permission. So he asked for it. He asked the king, the only one who could assist him with this need, "If it pleases the king, let letters be given to me for the governors of the region beyond the River, that they must permit me to pass through till I come to Judah" (2:7). The result? "And the king granted them to me" (2:8). There is a right way and a wrong way to attain goals. Nehemiah was successful because he did things the right way. He sought and acquired the necessary paperwork and the required documents of permission. A leader after God's own heart always adheres to the law, always follows the rules. In doing so he will receive God's blessing, and all that he achieves will bring glory to God and further His purposes—all because he did things God's way.

Don't be the leader who takes shortcuts, knowingly sidesteps rules, or turns a blind eye or deaf ear to something that is less than legal or honest. Be a leader after God's own heart. Don't try to wing it. Do your homework!

Acquisition—An effective planner acquires what is necessary to reach the goal. Right about now, given all that's happened in Nehemiah's interaction with the king, the faint of heart might back off and call it quits. After all, Nehemiah still had his head—he was still alive! And, as one of the king's most valued and trusted servants, he had successfully received permission to leave the king's service and travel hundreds of miles to a far-off province. He had even been given authority to travel through many countries on his way to Jerusalem. In fact, he was to be the envoy or representative of the king (5:14)!

But Nehemiah wasn't finished. He also needed materials for the rebuilding process. There were plenty of rocks for the walls, but what he needed was lumber. Timber was a very precious commodity. Trees were in short supply. From his careful planning, he knew that in order to build doors for the different gates, reinforce the city wall, and construct residences, he would need lumber.

Nehemiah's solution? He boldly asked King Artaxerxes for "a letter to Asaph the keeper of the king's forest, that he must give me timber to make beams for the gates of the citadel which pertains to the temple, for the city wall, and for the house that I will occupy" (2:8).

As you lead in your family, your business, your church, your group, your team, your community, determine to see your planning phase all the way through to the very end, to every last item needed. Think through every detail. Note everything needed. And know how you are going to acquire it. In the New Testament we find a parable spoken by Jesus that teaches us this same principle:

> Which of you, intending to build a tower, does not sit down first and count the cost, whether he has enough to finish it—lest, after he has laid the foundation, and is not able to finish, all who see it begin to mock him, saying, "This man began to build and was not able to finish"? (Luke 14:28-30).

Be wise! Count the cost before you begin to build. Plan and supply your projects to the last detail.

Provision—An effective planner knows the ultimate Source for all success. Having done so much to prepare for this opportunity with the king, you and I might expect Nehemiah to give himself a big pat on the back—a big, "Well done, old boy!"

But Nehemiah? No way! As a leader after God's own heart, he knew full well the Source of his strength and success. And he rushed to give credit where credit was due: "And the king granted them to me according to the good hand of my God upon me" (Nehemiah 2:8).

Nehemiah's dependence on God was real. And we'll see it time and again as we continue to look at his life. He was in every way a leader after God's own heart—the reason for the title of this book. Throughout the book of Nehemiah you will never witness the man taking credit for anything that happened. He knew God was behind it all, and his humility was genuine.

Nehemiah—a cupbearer, brother, and leader—provides a constant reminder that as you lead, you are not to boast of the things God does through you, as if you had accomplished them in your own strength and wisdom. A wise planner knows that even with all his planning and praying, it is ultimately God who makes the plan succeed. Only a fool believes he alone is the reason for his success.

The book of Proverbs affirms the provision of God in our actions:

> The preparations of the heart belong to man, but the answer of the tongue is from the LORD (16:1).

> A man's heart plans his way, but the LORD directs his steps (16:9).

Principles for Planning

Nehemiah, like most men, was not a soldier. Nor was he a religious teacher. So, for most men who are aspiring to leadership—that is, for those who aren't in the military or who aren't pastors—he is the perfect role model. Even though Nehemiah could fight if needed, and he probably could teach, his main contribution as a leader was more administrative in nature. He provides for us some valuable principles for the qualities of a good leader, and one of those qualities is that he was a good planner.

Planning involves a partnership with God. Nehemiah's consistent reliance on prayer is a loud indicator of the importance he placed upon his relationship with God. He knew He was fully dependent upon God for everything, and it showed in the priority he gave to prayer.

The proud can't pray. The self-reliant won't pray. But the humble of heart must pray. Nehemiah knew the only hope he had for his plans to succeed was God. Therefore he prayed.

Planning involves people. Nehemiah was a student of human nature. He didn't *use* people. But, as you'll see again and again, he *understood* them. He understood the king and how to approach him. He knew the king's plans and ambitions, problems and concerns.

Obviously, Nehemiah had become very trusted, respected, and dear to the king. But that didn't keep him from being extremely wise and sensitive in his approach to the king with his requests. By mentioning tombs and gates, Nehemiah painted a picture for the king of honoring the dead and restoring a society that was about to be destroyed for lack of protection. The king, someone his cup-bearer knew well and understood, could relate to national security!

Planning requires a complete set of plans. Nehemiah was focused and persevering. He left nothing to chance. He did not stop after the king had granted his initial requests. That's not what a leader does. So he continued until he received everything he needed to complete the job. Again, Nehemiah knew his king. And he knew how far he could press to get what he needed.

We don't know all the details of what was happening around this time in history throughout Artaxerxes' kingdom. But whatever it was, Nehemiah used it to appeal to the king so that he was able to get the king to agree to an almost impossible set of demands!

Planning may require the purposeful neglect of some things. Nehemiah could not do everything. He couldn't continue to serve the king *and* rebuild the wall. So he chose to focus his attention on one thing— rebuilding Jerusalem. That is, Nehemiah followed a course of "planned neglect." He chose to "neglect" other lesser things in order to accomplish one thing—the greater thing, the greatest thing.

I remember a story about a concert pianist who was asked about his secret to success. His answer was something like this: Planned neglect! When asked for clarification, he described how he first began to study the piano. He was young, and many things were demanding his attention. Each time he took care of other demands, he would return to his music. As it turned out, his music was getting the short end of his time—the leftovers. So one day he made a decision to deliberately neglect everything else until his practice time was completed. That program of planned neglect accounted for his success.

It's the same for you. You can't do everything. In fact, you cannot do *most* things. So you must implement a strategy of "planned neglect." You must plan to neglect nonpriority projects, issues, or activities in order to complete well those things that are the most important.

What is the one thing you want to—or must—complete or accomplish in the near future? Name it. Plan for it. And plan to neglect the lesser things along the way. Who knows? You too might build your wall, complete your project, and make your miracle happen just as Nehemiah did!

NEHEMIAH ON LEADERSHIP

It's obvious, isn't it, that Nehemiah was a passionate man? He could not have risen to such an exalted position unless he had been dedicated and passionate about his service to the king.

But now, he wanted—and needed—to focus his passion on one thing, on a new and more worthy objective—on rebuilding Jerusalem, the city of God. He spent months and months planning what was needed, planning on what to say, planning on what to ask for. At the same time, he chose to harness his emotions and wait and pray patiently for God's timing. He didn't try to break down any doors. He didn't try to push himself into the king's presence. He didn't try to rush the process through manipulation. But once God opened the door and created the opportunity, Nehemiah was thoroughly prepared to unveil his well-prepared plans with genuine passion and compelling persuasion.

How are you at balancing your passion while waiting on God's sovereign timing? How do you handle your great idea, dream, or noble cause with grace and patience when you've done your planning and are eager to persuade others to get on board? Follow Nehemiah's example. Temper your passion with an absolute confidence in God's ability to produce the desired outcome…in His time.

> *Wait on the LORD;*
> *Be of good courage, and He shall*
> *strengthen your heart; wait,*
> *I say, on the LORD!*
>
> (PSALM 27:14).

7

Motivation...Extends Your Leadership

I told them of the hand of my God
which had been good upon me, and also of
the king's words that he had spoken to me.
So they said, "Let us rise up and build."
Then they set their hands to this good work

(Nehemiah 2:18).

The journey from Susa was long and difficult. Even though the delegation had started the trip during the cooler spring months, the caravan trail had been hot and dusty. Nehemiah, the leader of the large group, had a lot on his mind during those hard months of travel. He wasn't concerned about bandits along the way. Why should he be? The king had gone so far as to graciously give him an escort of Persian troops!

With that potential threat taken care of, Nehemiah's brain was gnawing on two main concerns. The first was political. Every time his group passed into a new province, he had to stop and meet with the provincial leaders and notify them of his appointment as the new governor of Judea and seek approval to pass through their territory. While this protocol was necessary, it was also time-consuming, and Nehemiah was eager to arrive at his destination.

The second issue was practical. Nehemiah had been grateful for the king's stamp of approval on his mission. He was thankful, too, for the resources the king had provided. But there was still the question of the immense task ahead. How did he ever think he could make a difference? Conditions in Jerusalem had been grievous for nearly a century. Over and over he wondered, *Will I be able to achieve what I'm setting out to do? Am I getting into something bigger than I can handle? After all, no one else has been able to restore the city and its wall for several decades.*

These mental exercises continued throughout the journey, day after day, week after week. The thoughts continued circling in his mind even after his arrival. After three days of getting his troops and servants situated, Nehemiah decided to survey the rubble of the broken-down walls that surrounded the city of Jerusalem. He wanted to check out the situation in its entirety. Knowing of the opposing forces that surrounded him, he chose to take his survey at night to avoid notice. He had to see, with his own eyes, the extent of the damage and the amount of repairs that would be required for reinstating the wall.

Once Nehemiah's personal tour was done, his plans were finalized. He had anticipated this all along, but the truth came home to him as he saw the damage for himself. His survey had confirmed his suspicions that, even with all his personal resources and those provided by the king, he could not do this job alone. He would need the help of the people of the city and surrounding area. However, these same people had failed to do anything about the ruins for decades. This meant that somehow, he would have to motivate them and help them grasp how important it was to make Jerusalem safe and secure—to restore God's special city. *He* was excited. Now, the real task loomed before him: He would have to get the *people* excited too.

A Classic Example of Motivation

The date was June 4, 1940. World War II had descended Western Europe deep into darkness and chaos. Germany had brutally overrun several countries. London was being bombarded mercilessly. England had just pulled off a miraculous rescue of its entrapped Expeditionary Force from the beaches of Dunkirk in

France. With the army in defeat, the island of Briton was threat-ened with invasion. At this dark moment in history, a short stocky man—a leader—named Winston Churchill, who had just become prime minister of Great Britain, gave what is considered to be the defining speech of World War II. Through this speech he managed to instill strength and confidence in the people and rallied a belea-guered nation to fight on and ultimately win the battle. Here is a portion of his famous and inspiring speech:

> ...we shall not flag or fail. We shall go on to the end. We shall fight in France, we shall fight in the seas and oceans, we shall fight with growing confidence and growing strength in the air; we shall defend our Island whatever the cost may be. We shall fight on the beaches, we shall fight on the landing grounds, we shall fight in the fields and in the streets, we shall fight in the hills; we shall never surrender...

Churchill mustered the people from the brink of despair and destruction. The nation withstood terrible bombings and much more, yet she never gave up. In the end, Great Britain was victorious.

The Art of Motivating Others

Motivation can be defined simply as inciting others to action. That's what Sir Winston Churchill did. But how is this done? Lead-ers and companies use two primary forms of motivation: The first is *external motivation*. Outside force is applied to achieve a desired result from their people. They provide rewards like bonuses, all-expense paid vacations to exotic locations, corner offices, even keys to an executive washroom.

Those in leadership can also use external motivation in negative ways. They can threaten employees and followers with termination, the reduction of salaries, or demotions.

The problem with external motivation, whether positive or neg-ative, is that it only reaps short-term effects. All the bonuses or threats must be repeated again and again, only more so, in order to make those who would follow work harder for them.

Then there's the second form of motivation, *intrinsic motivation*. This has a stronger and more lasting impact. Intrinsic motivation appeals to the inner man—the heart. This was the main motivational style used by Churchill during the bleak and discouraging years of World War II. True, the fear of invasion was everpresent. But Churchill appealed to the fighting spirit of the British people. He challenged their national pride. He asked for their help in destroying evil.

It was intrinsic motivation that Nehemiah would use when he called upon the local residents in and around Jerusalem to rebuild the city walls and provide a safe haven for God's people. As someone has noted, "Leadership is the ability to get a person to do what you want him to do, when you want it done, in a way you want it done, because he wants to do it!"[19]

Setting the Stage

Nehemiah's journey from Susa to Jerusalem would have covered more than 900 miles. That means he traveled for at least two to three months—or maybe longer. Artaxerxes had provided him with armed troops for protection, and all along the way, Nehemiah showed the governors of various provinces the king's letters of authorization.

Nehemiah's checklist for undertaking the first part of God's assignment to him may have looked like this:

- Get king's permission—without losing my job or my life.
- Secure travel documents—to prove I am for real.
- Appease any potential enemies—while giving thanks for the king's supply of documentation.
- Accept king's gift of armed troops—they certainly would pave the way and make an impression!

- Make the long, dangerous trip to Jerusalem—and arrive alive and healthy.

With all of these goals and obstacles checked off, Nehemiah was soon to confront even greater challenges. He was facing a rebuilding project that had been neglected for some 90 years! In fact, after several infusions of Jewish people returning from exile, the wall and the city still lay in ruins. The people were living in survival mode, and no one had stepped up to do the task that so badly needed to be done.

No sooner had Nehemiah arrived in Jerusalem to contemplate and tackle the massive job of restoring Jerusalem than had word arrived of yet another challenge he would have to add to his checklist. Evidently the governor of nearby Samaria, named Sanballat the Horonite, was "disturbed that a man had come to seek the well-being of the children of Israel" (2:10).

Taking Command

Is there a right way to take up a new position of leadership? I'm sure you've witnessed a myriad of wrong ways to assume a new leadership role. People either love or hate the newbie, the one who takes up the reins. If the new leader comes in "with all guns blazing," someone is going to get hit! Unfortunately, it's usually the ones who don't deserve the hit.

Nehemiah was the newbie, the one who needed to take command. How was he going to approach this new-for-him role? Why not come in with the heavy hand? After all, he had the king's troops, the king's approval, the king's resources, and the king's timber. He could walk right in on day one and take control, right?

Yes, he could definitely do that. But in his mind, Nehemiah knew there was no way he could share with the people in Jerusalem what God was leading him to accomplish without first doing some personal research and planning. So, he took some time—three days, in fact—to pray (as always), to think, and to get acquainted with some of the people.

First he recruited a few men into his confidence, men he could trust. Then he made a careful survey of the walls to analyze the problems he faced. He did this at night, in stealth mode, apparently to avoid letting others know his plans before they were firmly fixed in his own mind. During that night tour he made a complete circle of the city and its broken walls (Nehemiah 2:11-16).

Becoming an Agent of Change

What did Nehemiah, a leader after God's own heart, do next? His heart was fixed. His mission was fixed. His facts were straight. Next he needed to motivate the people to want to do the work of resurrecting the stone wall around their city. Historians guess that the wall, to have fully encircled the city, would have to have been about 4.5 miles in circumference. (Many archaeologists believe that Nehemiah's completed wall was about the same size and length as the wall in Jesus' day.)

Maybe the people in Nehemiah's day were like so many of us today. There's just something about us that naturally makes us want to relax, rest, sit down with a good book, or watch a ball game (especially if our team is winning!). It's also our nature to prefer the status quo. We're resistant to change. We warn others, "Just don't rock my boat, okay?" And we think to ourselves, *I like things just the way they are.* We don't welcome the disruption caused by change—especially if we don't see a need for it.

Remember our definition of motivation? Motivation is inciting people into action, and that can include getting them excited about change. In Nehemiah's case, he had to first create dissatisfaction before he could incite others to action. He had to get them to realize their current situation wasn't good for them. Here's how one Christian leader states it:

> To increase motivation, a leader is required to stimulate people to a feeling of dissatisfaction with the status quo…The leader has to show the person how to apply himself to take the necessary actions to reach

the objective. A major stimulant is to arouse in the subordinates the feeling that success can be assured and that the task is important and carries a measure of status. Esprit de corps must be instilled.[20]

Motivation Starts with You

Creating dissatisfaction over a given situation starts in your own life. You cannot light a fire in another person's heart until the fire of your own heart is ignited. In order to motivate other people, you need to know how to get yourself in gear and start moving forward. If you want to instill intrinsic motivation—motivation from within—in others, then you must start with your own inner desire to press forward. You must first kindle a fire in your own heart.

There's no growth in the status quo. A life of ease and comfort may sound desirable, but slowly and steadily, you will surely shrivel up over time and die. Your potential will lose its momentum or diminish altogether. So to challenge and motivate others, you first need to challenge and motivate yourself. A challenge will cause you to grow. It will test your skills and hone your potential. A challenge can transform you from today's average guy to tomorrow's leader.

How can you create the challenges that will serve as the fuel for a life of self-motivation?

- Recognize your need to be challenged.

- Look around for what could qualify as a challenge.

- Identify the challenge and seek advice from literature, the Internet, professionals.

- Create activities for dealing with your challenge.

- Break your activities down into portions that are small enough so you have no excuse for not attacking your challenge.

- Establish checkpoints so you can assess your progress toward completing your challenge.

- Remind yourself of the benefits you can expect from completing the challenge.

- Recognize your limitations and set realistic goals.

- Take advantage of your energy peaks, those periods of the day when you are in top form.

- Take risks. Don't be afraid to take on something new.

- Use negative motivation by reminding yourself of the unfavorable consequences of the status quo.

- Set deadlines and hold yourself to them.

- Make an honest distinction between "I can't" and "I don't want to."

- Get started; don't stall.

- Be optimistic. You can do it!

Nehemiah wasn't entrapped in the doldrums of the status quo. Even though up to now he had lived in the king's palace and served him for some time, his life had not been one of ease. He had been challenged daily by his duties and responsibilities. In the king's service, things were always happening, so he had faced challenges on a regular basis. So when Nehemiah came to Jerusalem to challenge the people and secure their help, he wasn't asking them to do anything he wasn't willing to do himself. He was willing to accept the challenge and work right alongside them. As you'll soon see, Nehemiah personally led the charge to bring about the desired changes in Jerusalem, one challenge at a time.

Challenging the People

A former president of Columbia University once stated, "There are three kinds of people in the world—those who don't know what's happening, those who watch what's happening, and those who make things happen."[21] Obviously, Nehemiah was in the third group! After he completed his secret survey and developed a workable plan for restoring the city and wall, it was time for him to reveal to the Jewish people why he was in Jerusalem.

For this he assembled all the different classes of people who lived there—the nobles, the officials, and all the local citizens (verse 18). Then he laid before them his plan—a plan based on what he had seen and experienced during his first three days in Jerusalem. What were the elements of Nehemiah's approach to a skeptical and discouraged people?

He identified with the people—If a task is worthy, you must be willing to include yourself in the project. For instance:

- Nehemiah did not say, "I cannot do it alone."
- Nehemiah did not say, "I'll watch the work while you do it."
- Nehemiah used the secret weapon of motivation and said, "You see the distress that *we* are in...come and let *us* build" (verse 17).

He defined the problem—Often people are not properly motivated because they don't understand the problem. After all, these locals had lived in Jerusalem surrounded by deplorable conditions for more than 90 years! The inhabitants had given up long ago and become apathetic to their situation. Nehemiah knew the first step to change was to shock the people with a reality check. He pointed to and defined the problem: "You see the distress that we are in, how Jerusalem lies waste, and its gates are burned with fire" (verse 17).

He developed the plan—Sometimes the best plan is the simplest plan. Nehemiah didn't lay out a detailed architectural blueprint or a list of the how-tos of the project. He focused only on the end result: "Come and let us build the wall of Jerusalem" (verse 17). I can't help but say it: The wise man Nehemiah used the KISS principle: Keep It Simple, Stupid.

He described the purpose—Nehemiah exhorted the people to act, reminding them that they were held in contempt and scorn by their neighbors because of the run-down condition of their city. As their surrounding neighbors viewed their pathetic situation, they became filled with contempt not only toward the Jewish people, but also for their God (verse 19)! Nehemiah gave them a grand purpose: He appealed not only to their nationalistic zeal, but also to their religious spirit.

He detailed the power—In the end, Nehemiah bolstered his challenge with two further facts. First, he reminded the people that God's powerful hand had been with him and would continue to be a part of this project. Second, he reminded them that he was acting on the authority of the greatest physical power of that day, the king (verse 18).

How well did Nehemiah do his job of motivating the people to action? You already know, don't you? The Bible reports, "So they said, 'Let us rise up and build.' Then they set their hands to this good work" (verse 18).

Lessons on Motivation

Do you believe strongly about something—anything? If you believe strongly enough about something, you will not have to look very far to find others who are willing to follow. Nehemiah believed strongly about Jerusalem and the welfare of the people, and he found people to join with him in the cause he was promoting. So what can Nehemiah teach us about motivation?

Motivation begins with you—Be excited. When you are, others will get excited too. If you have a positive outlook—a can-do attitude about life and your mission—others will gladly join you in your venture. If you demonstrate confidence, others will feel confident in following you.

Motivation comes from within—Appeal to the inner man. If your followers catch your vision and internalize your cause, they will remain motivated when things get tough. Even when the bombs of setback are exploding around you, your followers will stay by your side as you strive to do what's best for all.

Motivation describes opportunities—Nehemiah did not become distracted by the difficulty of the project or the sacrifices that the people would have to make while rebuilding the wall. They had already been immobilized by high hurdles for 90 years. Instead, he directed their gaze to the golden opportunities of the future. He helped them to see solutions, not problems.

Motivation creates a need for change—A wise leader knows when it's time to move his people out of "the status quo zone" and on to a new challenge. Nehemiah pointed out the people's deplorable condition, called for change, and mobilized everyone to rebuild the wall and regain their national spirit.

Motivation points out resources—It's one thing to create a need for change, to give people the big picture—the *why* of what needs to be done. But without the *how*, there will only be frustration and discouragement. Nehemiah motivated God's people to act by supplying them with the *how*, the resources which included the king's approval and support. Make sure that whenever you need to motivate people, you give them both the *why* and *how*.

Motivation extends your leadership—You can accomplish a lot by yourself. But you are just one person, no matter how efficient, knowledgeable, and capable you are. By definition, a leader is one who leads...which means he has followers. But what kind of followers? And with what level of intensity? Motivation ignites people and turns them into a viable and explosive force that can work together to fulfill visions and goals. It's good to remember that an inability to motivate others is one of the main reasons those who are placed in leadership positions fail.

Nehemiah on Leadership

By steering the people of Jerusalem away from their fears and toward the Lord, Nehemiah fixed their minds on God and what He was doing for them. The people's reception to this news was incredible. For 90 years, whenever they were faced with the need to repair and rebuild the city and its wall, their response had been, "It can't be done!" After Nehemiah stirred the people's hearts and gave them a reason for strength and a purpose, the people united and became eager to begin the work of rebuilding the defenses of their city. They were incited toward action, saying and believing, "We can do it!"

What walls do you need to build or rebuild in your life? In your family or your world? What impossible task is looming on your horizon? Look at Nehemiah's example. Realize you can't succeed alone. Do your homework. Then go to the people who can labor with you to make it happen. Let them see your willingness to be involved. Convey your confidence in their ability. Enlist their support. Then challenge them to action. Like Nehemiah, if others see the strength of your excitement, they too will be strengthened and take action.

> *Motivation is human energy—the most plentiful*
> *and powerful resource on earth. It is the fuel*
> *that runs all social organizations from nations*
> *to families to individuals. We can never run out*
> *of it, yet we never seem to have enough.*[22]

8

DELEGATION...UNLEASHES YOUR LEADERSHIP

So they said, "Let us rise up and build."
Then they set their hands to this good work
(NEHEMIAH 2:18).

What was Nehemiah planning? What was the king's cupbearer-on-loan-to-Jerusalem up to? Exactly how would he approach the massive and seemingly impossible task of rebuilding the 4.5-mile-long wall around the city of Jerusalem? Didn't he know others had given up on any hope of doing this for 90-plus years? And that there were many who thought it simply was not possible?

Nehemiah knew all this. But it didn't stop him. It caused him to move forward with caution, but it did not weaken his resolve to rebuild the wall. After all, God had placed this noble task on his heart. Nehemiah hadn't heard any voices from heaven, nor had he been visited by an angel, but in his heart he knew he was doing God's will. God was asking him to do this, and that which God commands, He will give supplies for.

God's leader after His own heart's planning and praying was about to be tested. But wait a minute! Where exactly did Nehemiah's plan come from? Obviously, it didn't develop in a vacuum. Remember, Nehemiah was a prominent official in the palace of the greatest ruler of his day, Artaxerxes. And if Artaxerxes was like most kings, he was involved in a lot of building projects. If so, Nehemiah very likely had firsthand knowledge about how to go about carrying out this task. That's why, when the king asked Nehemiah what he needed, Nehemiah was able to give the king a very specific list of items he needed for rebuilding the wall.

Now, there were some very significant differences between what Artaxerxes had at his disposal and what Nehemiah had. For example, the king had a limitless supply of slaves to do his building projects. By contrast, Nehemiah had only the few people who had come with him. They weren't enough. Nehemiah needed the help of the local residents, yet he couldn't force them to labor with him.

What could he do, then? Enlist local manpower! *That shouldn't be a problem*, our leader thought, *since more than 50,000 men have returned over the past years. The real trick*, he realized, *is getting them motivated. Once that happens, I'll do what I've seen done in Susa. I'll assign different portions of the rebuilding project to different work-teams comprised of the local people. That will make the task more manageable for everyone.*

We don't know whether Nehemiah might have considered such a strategy while on the road to Jerusalem, or while surveying the wall under the cover of darkness during the three days before he gave his great motivational speech. But it was a strategy that made sense. What's more, Nehemiah further determined that people be assigned to the portions of the wall right where they lived! The manner in which Nehemiah planned what to do, motivated the people to do it, then delegated the parts of the project made the seemingly impossible become very doable. His approach sounds a lot like that of Henry Ford, the great automaker who said, "I am looking for a lot of men who have an infinite capacity to not know what can't be done."[23]

A Father-in-Law's Advice

How would you feel if, in the span of just a few months, you went from shepherding a flock of a few hundred sheep to shepherding a multitude of more than two million people? That was the predicament in which Moses, God's leader of the exodus, found himself. One minute he was looking at a burning bush in the desert, the next he was standing before one of the most powerful men on earth—the Pharaoh—and asking that all the Hebrew slaves in Egypt be freed to go into the desert to worship God. And that was only the beginning.

After God had intervened in some big ways and brought the people out of Egypt and into the desert, Moses got a new assignment: He was to guide this mass of humanity to the Promised Land. What approach would he take to governing such a large number of people as they journeyed to a new country?

It wasn't long before Jethro, Moses' father-in-law, heard what God had done to free the Israelites. Jethro then traveled from his home to meet up with Moses. After Jethro arrived, he observed that Moses was sitting from dawn to dark hearing the complaints of the people and judging their cases. This demanded all of Moses' attention and exhausted him—to the point he was unable to do anything else. Jethro offered his son-in-law some wise advice:

> You shall select from all the people able men, such as fear God, men of truth, hating covetousness; and place such over them to be rulers of thousands, rulers of hundreds, rulers of fifties, and rulers of tens. And let them judge the people at all times. Then it will be that every great matter they shall bring to you, but every small matter they themselves shall judge. So it will be easier for you, for they will bear the burden with you (Exodus 18:21-22).

Moses learned a valuable lesson on leadership and, more specifically, on delegation: A good leader does not do those things that can readily be assigned to others. Rather, he will delegate—and in doing so, he will raise up new leaders. And more importantly, this will free him to be fresh and creative when he does the bigger tasks that need his attention. He will not get bogged down in minute and unnecessary details. Jethro's advice would free up Moses to do what he needed to do most.

J.C. Penney, the founder of one of the largest department store chains in America—who was also a devout and outspoken Christian—was once quoted as saying, "One of the qualities I would look for in an executive is whether he knows how to delegate properly. The inability to do this is, in my opinion (and in that of others I have talked with on this subject), one of the chief reasons executives fail."[24]

The Fear of Delegation

It cannot be disputed that the leader who delegates work to others can often do that same work in a better and more efficient manner. However, when a leader tries to do all the work on his own, he ends up losing his focus and providing poorer leadership. Every leader needs to recognize he is limited in time, strength, and ability. (Just ask Moses!) That's why delegation is so important.

According to leadership expert Hans Finzel, a failure to properly delegate tasks is one of the top ten mistakes leaders make. Why is this the case? Here's the answer in just one word: *fear.*[25]

Fear of losing control—One of the qualities consistently seen in a good leader is that he is a "take charge" kind of person. He is a decision maker. A problem solver. The point man who provides direction for others. This works well as long as he can keep his arms around the project. If he's an exceptionally gifted leader, he can wrap his arms around most projects. Something may come along that almost kills him and the people on the project, but he gets it done by exercising good leadership qualities. Unfortunately those leaders with a "control issue"—that is, an inability to delegate and form teams—cannot take on very large projects. Because they are unable to delegate, they limit their range of effectiveness.

Fear of incompetence—For the most part, a leader is where he is because of his abilities. He has worked his way up the ladder, and now he's in charge. Because he knows what it takes to succeed, he is reluctant to allow others to assume much or any responsibility. He

fears the incompetence of others. He doubts their ability
dle the job, and is afraid he would have to step in later and clea
their mess. Because he's good at what he does, he can't or won't tru
others to help in the work of running the company.

Fear of losing recognition—There are lots of reasons people are driven
to do a job. Some thrive on the next bonus or raise, while others
thrive on recognition. They love the spotlight! They love being told
what a great job they are doing. It's understandable, then, why this
type of leader is reluctant to delegate to others—they might get
some of his praise and recognition!

Fear of needing others—The art of delegating requires involving other
people. It's an admission that others are needed to help get the job
done. Again, our Strong Natural Leader doesn't want or need others to help. As a SNL, he can do it himself. He got where he is by
himself, and he doesn't need anyone else to help, so he will simply
say, "Thanks, but no thanks." Delegation suggests a need for others. This stoic says, "I don't need help. I can suffer through it myself."

Fear of parting with knowledge—What is one of the most powerful tools of leadership? Knowledge! If you know something I don't
know, then you can control or direct me based on what you know.
That's why it's frequently said that knowledge is power. If a leader
believes this, then he's going to be reluctant to transfer some of that
knowledge/power to others. Oh, he might give out bits and pieces
of his knowledge so he can get a job done. But he will hold tightly
onto the most essential knowledge to ensure he retains as much
power as possible. Unfortunately, because he does this, those who
work alongside him get frustrated and are likely to fail because they
haven't been given everything they need to achieve successful results.

A New Testament Perspective on Delegation

Before we take a closer look at Nehemiah's process for delegating
work, let's see some examples of delegation in the New Testament.

...ation—Jesus knew His days on earth were
...w that before His death, resurrection, and
...eded to prepare others to carry on the work
...hy He chose and trained the 12 disciples.
...death, He gave them this mandate:

> ...therefore and make disciples of all the nations,
> baptizing them in the name of the Father and of the
> Son and of the Holy Spirit, teaching them to observe
> all things that I have commanded you; and lo, I am
> with you always, even to the end of the age (Matthew
> 28:19-20).

The apostle Paul and delegation—Delegation was to be the mandate
for the New Testament church, according to the apostle Paul. The
church was to know a shared leadership in which tasks were delegated, according to Ephesians 4:11-12: "[Christ] gave some to be
apostles, some prophets, some evangelists, and some pastors and
teachers, for the equipping of the saints for the work of ministry,
for the edifying of the body of Christ."

If you are a leader, it's vital that you equip others to lead. If you
are a follower, it is crucial that you develop your spiritual gifts so
that those in leadership can delegate the work of service based on
your gifts.

Your delegation at home—As a husband, learn to trust your wife and
delegate the responsibility of running the home in your absence. As
a father, train your children in the skills for running a home. Then
delegate those tasks and oversee their completion.

Beginning the Impossible Task

Now we're ready to go back to Nehemiah! A task so enormous
as rebuilding the walls of Jerusalem, especially under adverse conditions, called for unusual organizational skills. The plan and its
execution is found in chapter 3 of Nehemiah. There is no specific

notation that Nehemiah himself was the one who divided this large project into manageable pieces. However, it's hard to believe that the people took the initiative and organized themselves into work crews that would repair specific parts of the wall. So, consistent with his past record, let's assume that Nehemiah delegated the task of rebuilding the wall. Delegation goes beyond motivation. Motivation is creating a desire; delegation is pointing in a direction.

The delegating process can be seen as you read the phrases "next to them," "next to him," and "after him" 28 times in Nehemiah 3. Also, as you are reading along in this chapter, you will notice that each paragraph focuses on one of the ten gates of the city—such as the Sheep Gate, the Fish Gate, etc. If you consult maps of the ancient city, you will see that Nehemiah set up 42 crews to work around the entire city.

Here are some key points to observe about Nehemiah's delegation:

Assignments were made near where people lived. Nehemiah was aware of the enemies lurking nearby, so he assigned people to work on the sections of the wall nearest their homes. He knew if fighting broke out, each person would want to immediately defend his home and family. Also, setting up the assignments in this way would cut down on the amount of time people had to travel between home and work. This also allowed each head of household to involve his wife and children, making the work a family effort.

Assignments were made by vocation. The very first people mentioned in Nehemiah 3 are the high priest and his fellow priests, who worked on the Sheep Gate. These religious leaders would be particularly interested in the gate nearest the temple area, where animals would have been brought in for sacrificial offerings. Other workers whose vocations were listed were goldsmiths, perfumemakers, and merchants.

Assignments were given to outside inhabitants. Even those who lived in outlying villages joined in the work. Men from Jericho, Tekoa,

Gibeon, and Mizpah were assigned to sections of the wall where there were few homes.

What was the result of all this delegation? Nehemiah reports, "So we built the wall, and the entire wall was joined together up to half its height, for the people had a mind to work" (4:6).

Nehemiah on Delegation

One of the ways to be a strong and effective leader is to delegate. Here's an easy way to remember how Nehemiah shared the workload with others: D-E-L-E-G-A-T-E.

Determine the task. Not all of your responsibilities should be delegated. Select those tasks which could be successfully completed by others with less oversight on your part. Nehemiah knew the task before he left Susa. In fact he knew what needed to be done months before he arrived in Jerusalem because he prayed and planned ahead.

Examine the duties. Evaluate each task and determine what abilities, training, and gifts are needed. Can you give the whole task to one person, or a team? Do you need to assign specific people to specific projects? Nehemiah asked the people to take the responsibility for the part of the wall nearest to their home or place of work.

Leadership must be selected. Select the person with the greatest match of abilities, training, experience, and gifts needed to complete the task or be the point man who can ensure that others compete the project. As you read Nehemiah chapter 3 in the Bible, you'll notice that specific names are mentioned in relation to the section of the wall those people worked on. These people were the leaders of their families or clans.

Educate your leaders. Properly motivate and prepare your delegates for carrying out their assignment. Make sure they understand as much as you know about the task they are to do. There are no details as to what, if any, instructions Nehemiah might have given, but the leaders evidently knew what to do and how to do it.

Guide the leaders. Present them with a picture—either real or mental—of what your vision is for the project. Hand over the work for others to do, and don't smother them with your oversight. Identify key points or dates when you want feedback about their progress. It appears Nehemiah did this, for at one point he reported that the wall "was joined together up to half its height" (4:6).

Authorize the leaders. Give them the authority and resources needed to successfully complete the work. Once Nehemiah assured the leaders of the king's support and provided the provisions, the leaders took control and carried out the responsibilities assigned to them.

Trust the leaders. Encourage independence. Don't take back control. Give others the freedom to fail—or, as some people say, "Give them enough rope to hang themselves," so to speak.

Evaluate the progress. You know your desired outcomes. Next you need to ask, Is this task proceeding toward my desired goals? If not, what midcourse corrections might you suggest? If things are going according to plan, encourage, compliment, and offer your continued support for their leadership. Identify the measurements or outcomes you will use to determine whether the project was completed successfully—sales made, customers served, etc. In Nehemiah's case, it was the completion of the wall in 52 days. That's less than two months—what an incredible feat! Delegation made it possible—along with the "good hand" of the Lord (Nehemiah 2:8).

"The best executive is the one who has sense enough to pick good people to do what he wants done, and self-restraint enough to keep from meddling with them while they do it."[26]

NEHEMIAH ON LEADERSHIP

Nehemiah did not hesitate to relinquish control of the day-to-day oversight of individual building teams. He seemed to be a big-picture leader. This was possible only because he was willing to delegate.

How are your delegation skills? Do you identify with some of the fears mentioned earlier? You will never be a strong leader until you learn to delegate properly.

Are you convinced yet? Let's summarize the results of Nehemiah's delegation:

1. It increased his effectiveness.

2. It promoted leadership development.

3. It encouraged the sharing of wisdom.

4. It spread the burden of the responsibility.

5. It reduced the pressures of leadership.

6. It fostered decision-making.

7. It promoted personal growth.

8. It allowed for diversity.

9. It ensured his success (4:6).

> *The leader who creates, delegates, and moves on*
> *to still more creative activity will find himself*
> *or herself leading the pack. And the inability to*
> *delegate has been proven again and again to be the*
> *most common reason for leadership failure.*[27]

ENCOURAGEMENT...
SUPPORTS YOUR LEADERSHIP

Our adversaries said,
"They will neither know nor see anything,
till we come into their midst and kill them
and cause the work to cease"

(NEHEMIAH 4:11).

Nehemiah was pleased with the progress the people were making on rebuilding the wall. He marveled, *In spite of the continuous threats by their enemies, these people have stayed focused and kept up their work.* It was clear to Nehemiah that these residents of Judea now understood their sense of duty and the necessity of completing this important project.

But the threats were ever-present. What could Nehemiah do to sustain the people's spirits and retain their focus? "How can I encourage them in their work?" he muttered to no one in particular as he paced back and forth on the strategic towers that had been constructed to keep watch. *One thing is for sure,* he thought. *I can continue to pray for God's protection.*

In addition, I can make sure that both the workers and the enemy see me and my soldiers. The builders might not know I'm praying for them, but they can be encouraged by the visible presence of my military escort.

And sure enough, as Nehemiah and his troops patrolled the work sites, the workers looked on with smiles. And, while the threats persisted as the wall was being built, Nehemiah paced and prayed...and prayed and paced.

Encouraging a Nation

The American people were fearful and greatly discouraged. On the other side of the Atlantic, the German military machine had rolled across Western Europe and threatened England. Then on December 7, 1941, the nation suffered a surprise attack on Pearl Harbor. And following that attack, the Japanese overran country after country, island after island, in the South Pacific. From all indicators, it looked like the Japanese military was even preparing to invade Australia. But all this was about to change just nine months later. That's when the battle of Guadalcanal took place.

Before this battle, few people had ever heard of Guadalcanal, a tropical island in the southwest Pacific. But by the time it was over, many people across the United States were aware of the defense of Lunga Ridge on September 13 and 14, 1942.

Merritt Austin Edson was one of the unsung heroes of the battle for this small plot of land during those early days of World War II. His crowning glory and the battle for which he will long be remembered by Marines and a grateful nation was on Lunga Ridge, which has become known as Bloody Ridge.

Edson's Raider Battalion, with two companies of the 1st Parachute Battalion numbering about 800 Marines, repeatedly withstood the assaults of more than 2500 Japanese soldiers. The Japanese had yet to suffer defeat, so they were extremely confident of victory over this small resistance. Throughout the two days of intense and continuously vicious attacks, Colonel Edson walked along the battle lines continually exposing himself to enemy fire as he encouraged and reassured his young troops, who were mostly boys in their late teens. Edson's men sustained 256 casualties, but their tenacious and sacrificial stand ensured the taking of this island and the beginning of the end for the Japanese aggression.

Setting the Stage

When I first heard of Colonel Edson and his leadership during the battle at Lunga Ridge, I couldn't help but think of Nehemiah.

Edson's courageous stand reminded me of Nehemiah's diligent efforts to encourage his beleaguered people as they stood against the enemies who surrounded Jerusalem during the time the wall was being rebuilt.

The time came when all seemed to be going well on the rebuilding project. Most everyone was working together, side by side, unified in their objective. Progress was being made. The wall was taking shape. But the enemy's original opposition (2:19) began to accelerate as the reality of the project began to solidify. First there was mockery (4:2-3). Then they began to plot an attack against God's people (verses 7-8).

The Tool of Discouragement

It's a fact: You cannot constantly hear and be associated with threats and negativism without having some of it rub off on you in the form of discouragement. Discouragement is one of the greatest enemies of progress. It has kept even some of the greatest of projects from being completed. Discouragement has deadened the resolve of even the strongest of leaders and their people.

The fanciful story is told of a big rummage sale being held by the devil. He had neatly displayed many of his tools for public inspection, each with an accompanying price tag. Included were well-known tools like hatred, envy, jealousy, deceit, lying, and pride, among others. But laid apart from the others, as a special item all to itself, was a tool priced far higher than the others. A buyer pointed to this seemingly harmless but well-worn tool, and asked, "What is the name of this tool, and why is it priced so high?"

"This is discouragement," said the devil. "And the reason it is priced so high is because it is more useful to me than all the others!" The devil went on to say, "With this tool I can pry open a man's heart when I cannot get near him with any of the other tools. Once inside, I can make him do whatever I choose. It is badly worn because I use it on almost everyone. Few people know it belongs to me."

Reasons for Discouragement

Discouragement had been responsible for keeping the people of Judea from rebuilding their city for over 90 years. Even though they knew they had been miraculously repatriated to their land, and that God had promised to restore their nation, they were still frozen in inactivity. But Nehemiah had turned their long and deep-seated discouragement into excitement. And more important, he had turned it into hope. He had initially infused them with optimism regarding God's provision. He had given them a renewed sense of self-respect so they wouldn't be perceived by their enemies as weak and vulnerable.

But now that confident spirit was being threatened. The people were becoming discouraged in response to the threats of their enemies (verses 10-14). Here are some of the reasons they became discouraged. You can probably relate to many—or even all—of them.

Fatigue—"The strength of the laborers is failing" (verse 10). The word "failing" means "to stumble, totter, stagger." Working night and day had exhausted the people physically. Unfortunately when you are physically tired, you are more prone to becoming depressed, discouraged, or defeated. The famous football coach Vince Lombardi, the former coach of the Green Bay Packers, is said to have stated, "Fatigue makes cowards of us all!"

Loss of enthusiasm—"There is so much rubbish" (verse 10). With their physical strength failing, the builders began to lose their optimism and, therefore, their enthusiasm for doing the job. The halfway point is usually the most crucial time for any project, and the laborers were past this point. Their initial zeal had waned and they began to complain. Initially, the people hadn't complained about the rubbish. Now, with half of the wall complete, there surely must have been less rubbish! Yet it wasn't the debris that was the problem—it was their attitude.

Loss of vision—"We are not able to build the wall" (verse 10). The people originally had great motivation to build the wall. Nehemiah had convinced them that they could do the impossible. He had given them a goal, a direction, a reason for being. But in time, that vision grew dim. A loss of direction is always a big reason for discouragement. And it can happen to anyone. Losing one's way can create a sense of despair and hopelessness. This negative feeling has many names, like midlife crisis, or burnout, and in severe cases, depression. These people had lost sight of what they were working toward. Their myopia was not physical, but mental and emotional. They could no longer envision a finished wall. They could only see the rubble that still lay on the ground.

Loss of optimism—Nehemiah's workers heard the negative comments coming from their enemies. Very few people can stay optimistic when they're surrounded by negativism. They also heard intimidating rumors about how the enemy was planning to attack them: "They will neither know nor see anything, till we [their adversaries] come into their midst and kill them and cause the work to cease...they [the bearers of bad news] told us ten times, 'From whatever place you turn, they will be upon us'" (verses 11-12).

One way you can keep yourself from being discouraged by a negative person is to avoid that person at all costs. Encouragement is important because it keeps us going. A positive attitude is contagious. If you are prone to discouragement, then surround yourself with encouraging people, and let their optimism rub off on you.

Loss of trust—"Do not be afraid of them" (verse 14). For 90 years the people had been locked in fear. Then Nehemiah came along and eased their fears. They had started the work of rebuilding the wall with complete trust that God would protect them. Now they had again become cowed by the threats of the enemy. They had forgotten the Lord and His ability to protect them. They had taken their eyes off God and started looking around at their precarious position. (Sounds like the devil had been wielding his tool of discouragement!)

Loss of motivation—Unfortunately, forward movement is not always perpetual. Newton's first law of motion, which states that a body in motion will stay in motion, does not apply to human emotion. All the negative forces around the Jewish people were leading them right back into the pit of despair—right back where they were when Nehemiah arrived: to inactivity! Nehemiah was about to lose control of the situation. How would he deal with the people's fears, concerns, and unhealthy attitudes?

Nehemiah Encourages the People

What could Nehemiah do to ensure a high level of continued optimism among the people? After all, if the momentum was lost, it would be hard to re-excite the people. Progress would come to a standstill and conditions could return to those of the degrading past. How could Nehemiah help to encourage the people?

Nehemiah had options. For one, he could ignore the discouragement. He could hope it would go away. Well, unfortunately, discouragement is like getting a flat tire while driving. You can ignore it and continue to drive on it, but the tire will not inflate itself. Or, you can stop and fix it. That's exactly what Nehemiah did. As a leader, how did he go about "fixing" the people? How did he encourage them? How did he inflate their morale? Follow along to learn about his approach to handling discouragement.

A leader takes action—Nehemiah could see the people becoming discouraged, so he took decisive action. First, he did what he had always done in the past when a crisis was brewing—he prayed! Prayer is seen by many as no action. Many would rationalize that it's like sitting around doing nothing. They believe it's a waste of time. But Nehemiah knew he was in a spiritual battle. For him, the first step toward action for this and everything he faced was to pray.

Up to this point, Nehemiah has offered up three prayers to a sovereign God:

Prayer #1—When he heard the news from Jerusalem

regarding its desperate condition, he prayed four months for *direction* (1:5-11).

Prayer #2—After four months of praying, when Nehemiah was confronted by the king, he offered up a quick prayer for *strength and wisdom* (2:4).

Prayer #3—When faced by an enemy that mocked the Jewish people and plotted to attack, Nehemiah, the leader, prayed for *protection and retribution* against those who were threatening the building process. He laid the whole matter out before the Lord. For Nehemiah, prayer was the first priority (4:4-5,9).

A leader balances his options—Nehemiah did not stop with just prayer. Satisfied that he had first consulted with God about the problem, Nehemiah took strategic action. This is how a leader keeps things in proper balance. To pray and do nothing more presumes on God. To take action without prayer indicates a lack of faith. Nehemiah prayed *and* acted, finding the perfect balance. The result? "We set a watch against them day and night...I positioned men behind the lower parts of the wall, at the openings" (4:9,13).

A leader gets the people involved—Knowing of his people's fear, Nehemiah took further action by involving the people in their own self-preservation. What did he do? "I set the people according to their families, with their swords, their spears, and their bows...Those who built on the wall, and those who carried burdens, loaded themselves so that with one hand they worked at construction, and with the other held a weapon. Every one of the builders had his sword girded at his side as he built" (4:13,17-18).

Nehemiah turned the people's attention away from themselves and onto the enemy—away from their discouragement and self-pity and onto their goal of guarding their homeland.

A leader knows his people—When the burden was truly too heavy,

Nehemiah knew he needed to lighten the load. So he stopped the work and didn't start it up again until the immediate threat of the enemy and the discouragement had passed (verse 15). Sometimes the best way to encourage yourself or your people is to take some time off. This is a proven remedy for dealing with fatigue. There is an old Greek motto that says, "You will break the bow if you keep it always bent." Do you sense that those you lead are getting discouraged? Maybe your—and their—bow is too tight.

A leader communicates—Great leaders know how to encourage their people with inspiring motivational speeches. But there are many qualified leaders who aren't gifted with a natural charisma as speakers. However, they can still inspire their people. As far as we can tell, Nehemiah didn't give some great speech. We are told that he "looked, and arose and said to the nobles, to the leaders, and to the rest of the people..." (verse 14). He simply spoke what needed to be said. You can do the same—your people need words of encouragement from you. It might be as simple as "Keep up the good work!" Or "You're doing a great job!" Or, as Jesus said, "Well done!"

A leader refocuses—Incredibly, the people were preoccupied with the *rubbish* around their building project. They needed their attention refocused so they were looking to the Lord. So Nehemiah reminded the people of who God is and His greatness. He asked them to "remember the LORD, great and awesome" (verse 14). Many people who are discouraged are thinking mainly about one thing—themselves, and these people were no exception!

A leader reminds—Michael Griffiths wrote a book in the 1970s entitled *God's Forgetful Pilgrims*, with the subtitle *Recalling the Church to Its Reason for Being*.[28] Griffiths was reminding the church of its calling. Like Griffiths, Nehemiah knew he needed to remind the people of the reasons for their sacrifices. He knew when to infuse them with a fresh dose of motivation. So, once again, he appealed to their intrinsic responsibility to protect those who couldn't defend themselves. He urged the people to "fight for your brethren, your sons, your daughters, your wives, and your houses" (verse 14).

Commenting on Nehemiah's actions, one writer says, "Knowing how to diagnose a decline in morale and being able effectively to encourage and motivate our co-workers whether in a large corporation or in a church, in a hospital or on the mission field is one of the important factors in successful leadership."[29]

What was the fruit of Nehemiah's actions to encourage the people? "And it happened, when our enemies heard that it was known to us, and that God had brought their plot to nothing, that all of us returned to the wall, everyone to his work" (verse 15).

Dealing with Discouragement

Nehemiah's actions provide a great model for dealing with discouragement in others. And it's important to understand that discouragement is not a respecter of persons or rank. It is contagious and easily contracted. You might even have a case of it today! For an individual, discouragement is a paralyzing problem, but for a leader, discouragement is lethal. So it's vital to deal with it when it surfaces. Here are a few ways you can deal with discouragement in your own life:

Recognize its source—The devil? You will always be faced with pressures that could easily foster discouragement. The enemy of your soul would like nothing better than to take you out of the game and see you benched. And the tragic thing is, it isn't God who does the benching. No, it's *you!* You put yourself on the bench with immobilizing discouragement. So you must take the next step and...

Resist the temptation—It's easy to think negative thoughts. Like the people building the wall, you only see the rubble and feel overwhelmed by the task. Your mind begins to think, *I can't do this. It can never be finished. This project has too many things working against it... and me!* What does Peter say to do when you are tempted? "Resist the devil and he will flee from you" (James 4:7).

Regain your relationship—Have you taken your eyes off your Savior? The apostle Peter admonishes you to not only resist the devil, but to take the next step and "draw near to God and He will draw near to you" (verse 8). You draw your strength to lead from the Lord. If that relationship has been stifled, then your confidence and resolve have also been affected. A wise leader stays close to his Lord.

Remove those who spread seeds of discouragement—It's one thing to merely disagree, but when undue negativism is being promoted, it's time to deal with the dissension. Rather than allow for negative thinking and negative input, ask for positive options to any and all problems, which are really opportunities waiting to be resolved!

Remember your power—As a Christian, you have Christ's power working in and through you. Remember the promise of Philippians 4:13, which assures you that you can do all things through Christ, who strengthens you. Also, remember the power in your people. Maybe you are not delegating properly. *Your* power is limitless if you don't limit your people's power and ability to contribute toward getting the work done.

Refocus your direction—Have you lost sight of your goals and direction? The only cure for such discouragement is to refocus on why you started your project in the first place. Hopefully, you involved God in your original plan. You believed the plan was God's will. If you believed in it, then why should a few problems keep you from continuing to believe and continuing to carry it out with your original enthusiasm?

Respond to the encouragement of others—Often we think no one notices our discouragement. But those closest to us often do, just as the king noticed the sadness in Nehemiah. When others speak up, don't reject their encouragement. A wise leader recognizes his own limitations and tendencies and allows others to help him shore up these areas. Take the Bible's advice: "Encourage one another day after day, as long as it is still called 'Today,' so that none of you will be hardened by the deceitfulness of sin" (Hebrews 3:13 NASB).

NEHEMIAH ON LEADERSHIP

Nehemiah encouraged the people to look to the Lord and remember His greatness. He built up their confidence by wisely inviting them to have the right focus. He gave them hope and challenged them to a greater course of action. And he stood firmly with them during the rebuilding process. His strength became their strength, and together they believed they would do the impossible.

A good leader sustains hope by offering both words of encouragement and works of support. Think for a moment about how you can follow Nehemiah's example. Who needs a word or an act of encouragement from you today? A family member? A coworker? A fellow member at your church? Or maybe someone in your neighborhood? A little bit of encouragement can go a long way toward brightening someone's spirit and motivating them to press on.

> *Your positive attitude affects everyone around you. Your attitude determines much more than your expressions; your attitude determines your mood, your effectiveness, your thinking, your communications, your actions, and your fate. How positive is your attitude?*[30]

Positive Thinking.

10

PROBLEM-SOLVING...
REFINES YOUR LEADERSHIP

After serious thought, I rebuked the nobles and rulers,
and said to them, "Each of you is exacting usury
from his brother"

(NEHEMIAH 5:7).

A number of weeks had passed since the work to rebuild the wall had begun. Nehemiah was extremely encouraged by the progress. In spite of the brief bout with discouragement and the short break for rest, things were going pretty well. In fact, as he surveyed the construction, Nehemiah was pleased that the wall had been completely joined. There were no gaping holes!

"Foreman!" he called. "What is your estimation of the progress so far?"

The foreman, a trusted engineer Nehemiah had brought with him from Persia, paused for a moment as if he were doing some last-minute estimates in his head. He said, "According to my calculations, the wall is now half the height it will be at completion."

Before Nehemiah had time to revel in this good news, one of his servants came running up to him, stopping to catch his breath before he could speak. Nehemiah immediately noticed the concerned look on his face and asked, "I know that's the look of bad news. What is the next problem we need to solve?"

The Enemy Within

One evening when I was surfing back and forth between my

two favorite TV channels, the Weather Channel and the History Channel, I caught an interview with Peter Tompkins.

According to the History Channel, in 1944 the Office of Strategic Services (OSS) recruited Peter Tompkins, a correspondent for the *New York Herald Tribune* and CBS, to go to Italy as an undercover agent. The OSS was a US intelligence agency formed during World War II, and it was the precursor to the Central Intelligence Agency (CIA). This agency was formed to coordinate espionage activities behind enemy lines for the branches of the US military.

Tompkins was an obvious choice. Because he was fluent in Italian and possessed journalistic skills, he could listen, observe, and transmit valuable information for planning the invasion of Italy. Later, after the war, he would publish his diary, a book entitled *A Spy in Rome*. In his book, Tompkins described the events leading up to the Allies' taking of Rome. He detailed the cat-and-mouse games he and the Italian resistance played with the German SS. On several occasions he barely escaped capture.

What caught my attention were his comments about the real threat to the safety of his spy teams. To my surprise, Tompkins said it wasn't the Germans—it was the Italian people! Because the Italians were so fearful for their lives, they would readily betray anyone if it might help their own desperate situation. As a result, Tompkins related that there was no one the teams could trust, which made his work as a spy even more dangerous than the norm.

Setting the Stage

In our last chapter, we witnessed how Nehemiah dealt with discouragement caused by external influences. If you are reading along in your Bible and following this leader after God's own heart's experiences, you know we are now coming to Nehemiah chapter 5. Here, there is no mention of the kinds of thorns Nehemiah encountered in the previous chapters. Yet Nehemiah still has problems on hand. Enemies like Sanballat, Tobiah, and Geshem were watching while division and strife erupted within the Jewish community. You can imagine they were all delighted with the dissension from within and toasting their good fortune with the day's wine. They knew that internal strife could accomplish what they hadn't yet been able to do—stop the rebuilding process.

Nehemiah, like Peter Tompkins, was experiencing almost the same kind of threat, not externally, but internally, from his own people! As happened with the Italians and Tompkins, the Jews had become the enemy from within!

To be more precise, the Jewish nobles now had become thorns in Nehemiah's side. Scripture notes: "Their nobles [the wealthy] did not put their shoulders to the work" (3:5). Their commitment to the work was negligible, and they had an allegiance to Tobiah, one of Nehemiah's chief enemies (6:17-19).

Now, even without the help of the nobles, things were beginning to look up. Progress was being made on the wall. But an underlying problem was about to surface. After years of defeat and discouragement, the land of Judea was in economic ruin. Even under "normal" conditions, poverty and starvation were all too common. And with the intense focus on rebuilding the wall, people were unable to work in the fields enough to support themselves and their families. Three groups were hit especially hard. After a time, they approached Nehemiah in desperation:

Group #1—These people were the laborers who worked the fields or jobs in the city. Because they had families, they were in urgent need of food. They didn't own property against which they could borrow money for food. Their resources were gradually used up while they worked on the wall. They were on the verge of rebellion, saying, "Let us get grain, that we may eat and live" (5:2). Reading between the lines, their desperation might be translated, "If we are not given some food, we will take it by force rather than see our families starve!"

Group #2—These people owned a little property but were forced to borrow money on their land so they could buy food (verse 3). Because of the presence of enemy forces surrounding them and the pressing need of manpower for rebuilding the wall, a famine was developing, and these small landowners were suffering. Historically and biblically, the Jews had a strong attachment to family property, and having their land and homes repossessed would be a national tragedy.

Group #3—These people had borrowed money to pay their taxes by pledging their crops which had not yielded enough to repay their creditors. Subsequently they had lost their fields and vineyards. Life and finances had gotten so bad they were even forced to sell their children into slavery (verses 4-5).

Internal Strife—An Age-Old Problem

A well-known cartoon character by the name of Pogo was once drawn standing on a rock in a George Washington pose, wearing a paper hat in the style of the Revolutionary War period, holding a small wooden sword in his outstretched hand, and exclaiming loudly, "We have met the enemy, and they is us!"

Pogo's declaration illustrates the point that we are often our own worst enemy. Internal strife has been around ever since groups first came into existence. Here's how some men—and leaders—in the Bible handled the problem of internal strife:

Abraham—The father of the Jewish people, Abraham, is an example of a leader after God's own heart. Genesis 13 tells the story of a problem that occurred between his herdsmen and those of his nephew, Lot. You might label this struggle the First Recorded Range War. Abraham saw very quickly that this internal strife could not continue. Abraham and Lot were guests of the Canaanites and the Perizzites (verse 7). If this problem was not handled properly, it would become a scandal that threatened to tarnish the name of God, whom Abraham was known to worship. Abraham defused the tension by offering Lot his choice of the land that was available. He let Lot choose the best grazing land in the area, and accepted the rest for himself. Problem solved!

Peter—This apostle was key to solving a serious problem in the early church. Christianity began as an offshoot of Judaism. For some years, most of the converts were of Jewish descent. But after Peter received a vision from God and was sent to a Gentile's home to share the gospel, an entire household of Gentiles became Christians (Acts 10). Peter came to realize God wanted to draw Gentiles to Christ too. During this time, the church in Jerusalem was being persecuted, and this persecution caused the Christians to scatter to Gentile lands, thus spreading the gospel.

Some years later, there was growing dissension in the church at Jerusalem. Some said that true believers must live by the law of Moses—that is, Gentile believers had to follow certain Jewish observances, including circumcision. Others, however, said salvation was by God's grace alone, making it unnecessary for Gentiles to follow certain Jewish laws and traditions. You can read the full story of this faith-battle in Acts 15.

Peter, the Jew's Jew, stood up and related how he had formerly been fearful about approaching the Gentiles with the gospel. But, to his surprise, they too had received the Holy Spirit in response to his preaching. The apostle Paul also offered a defense affirming salvation by grace alone. As a result, the apostles and elders affirmed that the Gentiles could receive God's grace in the same way as the Jews. They concluded that whether Jew or Gentile, all are saved by faith in Jesus Christ alone. Peter's speech was a turning point in the advancement of the gospel.

Paul—Though Paul was Jewish, he had an extensive ministry to the Gentiles. Some time after the critical Acts 15 meeting in Jerusalem, Peter visited the church where Paul was ministering. While there, Peter freely associated with the Gentiles in the church as fellow brethren. Then some people called Judaizers—people who felt Gentile believers had to follow Jewish laws and customs—came to Antioch. Amazingly, because Peter wanted the approval of these Judaizers, he withdrew from fellowshipping with the Gentile believers, even though he knew that in Christ, they were equals.

Because Peter was a prominent leader, his poor example influenced others to shun the Gentiles. This was truly a dark hour in the history of the gospel. How did Paul, a leader in this particular church, deal with the strife and division?

Paul could have been intimidated by Peter, but he refused to ignore the problem. He faced it head-on. With complete forthrightness he confronted the great apostle Peter. Peter then repented of his hypocritical actions and acknowledged the truth of the gospel—that Christ's saving grace extended to everyone who believed. You can read Paul's full account of this in Galatians 2:11-14.

Solving the Problem of Internal Strife

With these biblical examples fresh in your mind, let's return to Nehemiah. In the previous chapter, we read about Nehemiah solving problems that resulted from external threats. In this chapter, we see Nehemiah turning his attention to problems from within.

As Nehemiah heard the woes of these three groups of destitute people, he became "very angry" (Nehemiah 5:6). Why? Because part of the blame for the plight of these people was placed at the feet of their rich fellow Jews (verses 1,7). The nobles and rulers had taken advantage of the poor by charging excessive interest on the money loaned to them. Nehemiah called it "exacting usury."

According to Mosaic law, the Jews were forbidden from collecting interest from each other on the loan of money, food, or anything else. If a person was destitute, Jews were commanded to give what was needed as a gift. If the poor could pay the loan back later, the lender was to charge no interest. Lenders could charge interest only on loans to foreigners—not to fellow Jews.

Now can you see why Nehemiah was angry with the nobles and the rulers? With such rampant internal division and strife, it's no wonder so little progress was being made toward rebuilding the wall. And Nehemiah was faced with a very difficult problem. Should he side with the rich and influential? After all, he needed their support. Or should he take sides with "the little man"? Was Nehemiah a man of the people, or not? What should he do? Here's how he solved the problem:

Nehemiah defined the problem carefully (verses 1-5)—First, Nehemiah had to stop and listen to the complaints of the people. Now problems usually crop up at the most inopportune time, and this was no exception. Nehemiah was busy with a massive building project. The enemy was lurking just beyond the rubble. How could he take the time to listen? But, as an astute leader, he did take the time. His priorities were people first, project second. He probably imagined what might happen if the problem were left unsolved. He realized he could easily end up with a revolt on his hands, or, at the least, a drastic slowdown of the rebuilding process.

As Nehemiah listened to all sides, he began to get a clearer picture of the heart of the issue. The problem was not starvation—that was only a symptom of a bigger problem. The root problem—the real problem—was money, or greed! The rich were taking advantage of the poor, charging high interest rates without regard to what was prescribed according to the Mosaic law. That this resulted in complaints and frustration shouldn't surprise us. When it comes to leading people, we need to stay alert to the fact that many problems usually have money involved in some way.

Nehemiah dealt with the problem frankly (verses 6-7)—Some leaders are pros at avoiding an issue. They excuse it. They ignore it. They redefine it. They delegate it. They do everything they can think to avoid facing a problem, hoping it will go away. These leaders, unfortunately, lack the strength of character necessary to confront and solve problems. Nehemiah, however, faced the problem of usury head-on. He did not rush in. He took time to think over the issues. Then, "after serious thought," he acted: "I rebuked the nobles and rulers, and said to them, 'Each of you is exacting usury from his brother.'"

Nehemiah discussed the problem fully (verses 6-10)—Nehemiah evaluated the problem in the light of God's Word. Then he called a great gathering to discuss the matter with all the people. He challenged the nobles to obey God's law and standards, and to restore what they had taken from their Jewish brethren. He urged them to do what was right, for their greedy practices were bringing reproach upon God.

Nehemiah solved the problem successfully (verses 11-13)—Nehemiah set a good example for everyone by committing that he himself would make loans without exacting usury. Good leadership starts at the top. You cannot ask others to do something you're not willing to do. By setting an example and strongly encouraging others to do the same, Nehemiah was able to bring the problem to a right and satisfactory conclusion.

In the end, all the assembly said, "Amen!" and praised the Lord. Then the leaders did what they had said they would do: They restored all the interest on the loans and required nothing from the poor.

The Wrong Way to Handle a Problem

Nehemiah demonstrated the right way for a good leader to handle a difficult issue. By contrast, Aaron, Moses' brother and second-in-command, is a sad example of how not to handle problems. While Moses was on Mount Sinai receiving the Ten Commandments from God, Aaron was left in charge of the people of Israel. During Moses' 40-day absence, the people became impatient with a God they could not see. They wanted Aaron to help them make a god they *could* see. They cried out to Aaron, "Come, make us gods that shall go before us; for as for this Moses, the man who brought us up out of the land of Egypt, we do not know what has become of him" (Exodus 32:1).

Aaron was unwilling to face the problem or even try to persuade the people that making a idol was a bad idea. Instead, he took the easiest road to "solving" his problem—he gave in! But frequently the easiest solution is the wrong one. Aaron told the people, "'Break off the golden earrings which are in the ears of your wives, your sons, and your daughters, and bring them to me'…He received the gold from their hand, and he fashioned it with an engraving tool, and made a molded calf" (verses 2,4).

Aaron solved his dilemma in an irresponsible, cowardly manner. As a result of his failure to deal with the problem correctly, thousands of people died in God's ensuing judgment.

The lesson from Aaron's failure as a leader is sobering. It teaches us that every problem must be handled with care and courage. What may seem like a minor issue can easily escalate into a major crisis if it's not handled properly. When you have a difficulty to solve, approach it as if its solution will be life-altering. Chances are high that it will be!

A Leader's Skill in Problem Solving

Problem solving is one of the hardest tasks a leader faces. It is never "by the numbers" or "by the book." Each problem is unique. To deal with them successfully, you are required to think! Whether it's deciding which house to buy, the right school for your kids, the best vendor for your company, or simply choosing where to spend your next vacation, you need to take time to make right decisions. Here are a few basic steps for developing good problem-solving skills.

View each problem as an opportunity. Problems are the price of progress, whether it's having enough money to afford a new house or to take a vacation, or the need to find vendors for your growing company. Once you develop the mind-set that problems are opportunities, you will welcome them as chances for growth. You'll approach them with an attitude that says, "Here's my next opportunity!"

Problems provide you with the chance to refine your leadership skills. The process of solving them can bring up solutions that make you a better person and benefit others. Best of all, they allow you to demonstrate your faith and trust in God.

Acknowledge the problem. Most problems don't just go away on their own. That's why they are called problems! Now that you view problems as opportunities, whenever one arises, your immediate response should be to acknowledge and own it. This, in turn, will start the process of discovering what great new adventure is lurking behind this difficulty. General George S. Patton, the great World War II leader, was known for his ability to recognize a problem and deal with it. One biographer wrote, "Patton watched and drew conclusions. He had an uncanny ability to go straight to the heart of the problem and then intervene personally to correct it. He attended immediately to any problem he saw."[31]

Define the problem. Approach each new problem without bias. Don't be intimidated by those who may be causing the difficulty. Your job is not to appease, but to ensure that in solving the problem, you don't make things worse. Remember Aaron? What is the real issue? Instead of correcting the people and getting them to respond properly to God, he gave in and allowed them to worship an idol.

When you attempt to figure out the cause of a problem, you may not always like what you find, but that's part of being a good leader. You are not to find the easiest way out, but to ascertain the truth. Once you have defined the true facts of the problem, you can start moving toward a real solution. It's been said, "A problem defined is half solved." So when you define what's at issue, you're halfway to the solution. You can now determine what to do next. Don't deceive yourself, for there may be times when *you* are the problem!

Develop solutions to the problem. Once you have discovered the source, cause, or specifics of the problem, you are ready to delineate steps that must be taken to solve it. And don't forget, the problem you are facing has been faced by countless others before you. As Ecclesiastes 1:9 says, there's nothing new under the sun. Don't re-invent the wheel! As you look for solutions, if at all possible, seek the advice of others who have experienced the same problem and dealt with it successfully.

Resolve the problem. This sounds easy, but you won't be able to do this until you have prayerfully and thoughtfully walked through the process of figuring out the right steps to take. As you compare the consequences of your different solutions, you will be able to determine which one or ones work best in light of the people involved or the outcome for the organization as a whole.

NEHEMIAH ON LEADERSHIP

One of the ways a leader defines himself is in his ability to successfully solve difficult issues. The strength of a leader is determined by his willingness and ability to roll up his sleeves, get down in the trenches, and tackle life's toughest problems successfully. The tougher the problem, the more involved and deeper into the trenches a great leader is willing to go to provide solutions.

Nehemiah certainly demonstrated his skills in problem solving on many fronts. First, there was the problem of rebuilding the wall. He had been working on this since he had heard the news while in Susa. There was also the difficulty of external pressure from nearby enemies. Now there was the problem of internal strife between the nobles and the people.

Like Nehemiah, you will face many problems. They can't be avoided, and most can't be delegated. Your leadership—or your lack of it—will determine the final outcome of the problem. You need to take the same first step Nehemiah did—consider the resources you have for solving the problem, and the biggest one, of course, is God, the ultimate problem solver. As Nehemiah did, start with prayer, asking God for His wisdom. Then turn to your associates for their insights, ideas, experience, and wisdom. Take your time as you thoroughly evaluate your options. Then, with the best information and wisdom you have been able to gather, take action, and trust God for the results. With regard to considering your options and going into action, General Patton said this:

> *The best policy is to delay the decision as long as possible so that more facts can be collected. But when the decision has to be made, we will never hesitate.*[32]

11

CONFLICT MANAGEMENT...GIVES RESOLVE TO YOUR LEADERSHIP

"It is reported...the Jews plan to rebel...
that you may be their king"...For they all were trying
to make us afraid, saying,
"Their hands will be weakened in the work..."
Now, therefore, O God, strengthen my hands
(NEHEMIAH 6:6,9).

Nehemiah had done his homework. After hearing the report about the deplorable conditions in Jerusalem, he had spent his free time seeking recorded information about Jerusalem itself. In time he uncovered communiqués from as far back as 90 years that chronicled the slander campaign that had plagued the Jewish community around Jerusalem.

Sure enough, the ancestral conflict between the Jews and their neighbors had at times been vicious. One report even described how, during that time, the neighbors surrounded Jerusalem and forced a halt to the work of rebuilding the temple. As Nehemiah continued to sift through the reports, he eventually discovered some good news. He was thrilled to learn that, after 16 years and in spite of continued opposition from the region's enemies, God had miraculously intervened and overruled all opposition, and, praise be to God, the temple had been completed!

These truths served as a reality check for Nehemiah and provided hope for him while on the road to Jerusalem. He often thought, *I wonder what opposition I'm going to face? And what slanderous reports are God's enemies going to circulate about me? What devious plans do they have to keep me from doing this great work?*

Nehemiah knew that when he arrived in Jerusalem, he had a political hornet's nest looming before him. The conflicts of the past had not been resolved. The tension between the Jewish people and their neighbors still simmered. *How am I going to handle any new conflicts that arise?* Nehemiah wondered. *Only God can provide a miracle to resolve any difficulties we face. Please, Lord!* he prayed.

The Age-old Presence of Conflict

If you look up the word *conflict* in just about any dictionary, you will read a definition to this effect: A state of open, often prolonged fighting; a battle or war. A state of disharmony between incompatible or antithetical persons, ideas, or interests; a clash, a psychic struggle, often unconscious, resulting in mental anguish and possible open hostility.

Let's face it—as long as there is sin in the world, conflict will be a fact of life. Conflicts and their resultant wars have been a noted fact since the beginning of recorded history. The Bible documents its share of past conflicts in all their unvarnished reality. Here are several:

Cain and Abel—This conflict was between an envious man and God. Cain was upset because God accepted the sacrifice offered by his brother Abel, yet rejected Cain's sacrifice. The issue was between him and God. But instead of going to God to resolve the matter, Cain chose to confront his brother. Cain seemed to think God's response was Abel's fault. In a fit of anger and jealousy, Cain rose up and murdered his brother (Genesis 4:1-8).

Moses and Pharaoh—This conflict was between a proud man and God. God sent Moses to Pharaoh with the request that the Israelites be allowed to go into the desert and worship Him. Pharaoh and the Egyptian people had become dependent on the Jews as slave labor, so Pharaoh didn't want to honor the request. Also, Pharaoh believed his gods were stronger than Moses' god, and his pride caused him to repeatedly refuse Moses' request. After ten plagues and the near destruction of the land of Egypt and its people, Pharaoh finally relented, only to regret his decision. The final point of conflict came as the Pharaoh's army chased after the fleeing slaves, and was miraculously destroyed by God as the Red Sea swallowed the soldiers up in death (Exodus 5–14).

Miriam, Aaron, and Moses—This conflict arose on account of ambition. Moses' brother and sister used Moses' marriage to an Ethiopian woman as a pretext for an attack on Moses' leadership of God's people. They were envious of his position and his relationship with God. The Lord took offense with their actions against Moses and struck Miriam with leprosy (Numbers 12).

Those are just a few examples of the conflicts described in the Bible. As we once again turn to the life and leadership of Nehemiah, we see that he too experienced his share of conflicts. How he managed them tells us volumes about his skills as a leader. He teaches us how to manage the conflicts we face at home and at work, both now and in the future.

Nehemiah Faced Conflict

Nehemiah's efforts to rebuild the Jerusalem wall would defiantly threaten the status quo, especially for the enemies of God. The evil people who surrounded Jerusalem were desperate to keep the wall from being rebuilt. They wanted to keep the Jews weak and defenseless. The enemies pressed their conflict by opposing Nehemiah on six occasions, using six different means of attempting to stop the work on the wall.

1. Ridicule

Sanballat, with his Samarian army, had allied himself with Tobiah, the Ammonite. From a position of strength, they mocked Nehemiah's efforts on two separate occasions (2:19; 4:1-3). Initially, they laughed (2:19). This first response to the news of the rebuilding efforts was in the form of ridicule and mockery. But with each passing day, and as each stone was laid, God's enemies became more serious in their attempts to stop the wall from being built.

History has proven over and over that anytime the status quo is threatened, conflict soon follows. People are comfortable with what they know, even if it's not ideal. Conversely, people are threatened by the unknown. Vision and the prospect of advancement have often produced laughter and derision, at the very least. For instance,

> The first American steamboat took 32 hours to go from New York to Albany. *People laughed.* The horse and buggy passed the early motorcar as if it were standing still. (It usually was.) *People laughed.* The first electric light bulb was so dim people had to use a gas lamp to see by it. *They laughed.* The first airplane came down 59 seconds after it left the ground. *People laughed.*[33]

Nehemiah's response to his enemies' ridicule? "Hear, O our God, for we are despised; turn their reproach on their own heads" (4:4).

2. Open threats

Nehemiah's enemies—who were also enemies of God—had darker plans than merely sitting back and mocking and ridiculing the Jewish people's attempts to rebuilt the wall. As the building progressed, they intensified their opposition by threatening a military attack (4:7-23).

Nehemiah gave a twofold response to these threats. First, he placed men in the gaps. "I positioned men behind the lower parts of the wall, at the openings and I set the people according to their families, with their swords, their spears, and their bows" (4:13). Then he reminded the people of the power of their God, of exactly who was protecting them, and in turn, who they were to protect: "Remember the LORD great and awesome, and fight for your brethren, your sons, your daughters, your wives, and your houses" (4:14).

3. Diversion

"Sanballat and Geshem sent to me, saying, 'Come, let us meet together among the villages in the plain of Ono'" (6:2). One of the most effective military strategies is diversion or misdirection. The object is to get your enemy thinking in one direction while you move in another. In the corporate world this is sometimes called *distraction* or *majoring on the minors*. When you become distracted, you lose your focus and end up going in the wrong direction. That, in turn, causes you to lose your momentum on whatever you're doing.

If your opposition or your own lack of discipline end up getting you sidetracked from the tasks that are of real importance, then real progress will be lost. That's why it's vital to have goals. They allow you to constantly check yourself to see if you are being diverted by anything or anyone. Nehemiah knew his goal, and nothing was going to divert him from that. He was not going to lose his resolve. Note what he says—that his enemies "sent me this message *four times*, and I answered them in the same manner" (verse 4). When the enemies persisted, so did Nehemiah. He didn't quit. He said, "I sent messengers to them, saying, 'I am doing a great work, so that I cannot come down. Why should the work cease while I leave it and go down to you?'" (6:3).

4. Slander

Having again failed to achieve their purpose, Sanballat and his coconspirators tried a new strategy—slander. They sent an open letter to the public, a letter of proclamation, in which they charged Nehemiah with treason: "It is reported among the nations, and Geshem says, that you [Nehemiah] and the Jews plan to rebel... that you may be their king" (6:6).

Unfortunately, slander is often an effective weapon. Even if the allegations are unfounded and later proven to be false, its initial impact can cause a lot of damage. The slander from Nehemiah's enemies had the potential to sufficiently impugn his motives, cast suspicion on his integrity, and undermine his influence. The enemies took advantage of an important psychological principle—people are always quick to believe the worst about others.

How did Nehemiah respond? First, he sent them a letter of denial: "Then I sent to him [Sanballat], saying, 'No such things as you say are being done, but you invent them in your own heart'" (verse 8). And he declared that he knew their intentions: "They all were trying to make us afraid, saying, 'their hands will be weakened in the work, and it will not be done'" (verse 9). Nehemiah had no concern for their slander; he knew it was their way of trying to stop the progress on the wall. In fact, Nehemiah did as he had always done when confronted with a problem—he prayed. He didn't offer up a long prayer; rather, he was succinct and to the point: "Now therefore, O God, strengthen my hands" (verse 9).

5. Treachery

You could also call this type of opposition "false counsel or bad advice." When the open letter failed to stop the work, Nehemiah's enemies try yet another tactic—intimidation from within. They hired a false prophet (verse 12) to lure Nehemiah to the temple for protection because of all the threats on his life and reputation (verse 10). However, if Nehemiah were to enter the temple, he would have desecrated the house of God, for Nehemiah was a lay person, not a priest. Such an action would have caused all the people to question his reverence for God. His enemies could then give an evil report of his unlawful conduct (verse 13).

Nehemiah's response? First, he perceived that the counsel was false. He figured out what his enemies were attempting to do. Then he prayed: "My God, remember Tobiah and Sanballat, according to these their works, and the prophetess Noadiah and the rest of the prophets who would have made me afraid" (verse 14).

6. Subversion

Not to become paranoid, but a leader always needs to watch or have someone watch his back. "Great news!" shouted the messenger.

"The wall is finished." Nehemiah released a huge sigh of relief. He could finally take a bath! He had practically slept in his clothes through the entire 50-plus day ordeal. He could hardly believe it. In just 52 days the wall had been finished. *Finished!* And it was even reported that the enemy had finally become "disheartened" (verse 16). Nehemiah could finally relax and let his guard down, right? Wrong!

No sooner did Nehemiah begin to rejoice than he heard reports that "the nobles of Judah sent many letters to Tobiah and the letters of Tobiah came to them. For many in Judah were pledged to him, because he was the son-in-law of" the high priest (verses 17-18). Behind Nehemiah's back, letters were being sent and oaths were being made. His movements were being tracked and reported to the enemy. In other words, a fifth column, a subversive element, was in his midst! The nobles who had refused to work and had charged excessive interest on loans were also trying to play both sides.

Nehemiah's response? He didn't react. He simply acknowledged their plot: "They reported his good deeds before me, and reported my words to him. Tobiah sent letters to frighten me" (verse 19).

Principles of Conflict Management

Conflict is a fact of life. It will always be lurking around some corner. Your dreams and goals will often be met with opposition. As a leader, your job is to learn how to manage your ever-present— and often unpleasant—conflicts.

Here's a key point: You are never going to please everyone. The only One you must please is the Lord. Still, as a leader who serves Jesus, realize that He would want you, as much as is possible in your power, to be an instrument of reconciliation and to be at peace with all men (Romans 14:19).

Even if you possessed the wisdom of Solomon and the patience of Job, you will still have to struggle with conflicts. And as a leader, you can expect that many of the conflicts you face will originate with your associates and acquaintances. How can you resolve them? Nehemiah is a fantastic role model for conflict management, and here are some key principles we can learn from his example:

Accept conflict as a reality. As long as there are people with differing opinions, differing expectations, and differing goals, there will always be conflict. So expect disagreements. And don't ignore them when they surface. When Nehemiah set out for Jerusalem, he probably anticipated that he would face conflicts. After all, he had read about the centuries-old animosities that had flared up between the Jewish people in Jerusalem and the surrounding neighbors.

Realize a conflict doesn't have to bear negative results. Most of the time we see conflicts as negative. Tempers flair. Relationships are strained, or even broken. Little if any good comes from disagreements. But a conflict doesn't have to be seen as bad. It can produce growth and energy that can be channeled in a new or better direction. For example, suppose two scientists have a conflict over a new theory. If their conflict can be channeled in a unified direction, a better result can be accomplished than if either scientist worked by himself. Your job as a leader is to manage conflict so it is channeled in a positive direction.

Confront conflict quickly. Conflict is frequently the result of unresolved issues in relationships. Go to those who are causing the conflict. Address any issues with an open mind. Tackle it head-on, face-to-face, and handle it quickly. Stay focused, and make resolution a top priority. As Jesus said, "If you bring your gift to the altar, and there remember that your brother has something against you, leave your gift there before the altar, and go your way. First be reconciled to your brother, and then come and offer your gift" (Matthew 5:23-24).

Determine the basis of the conflict. What is the reason for the conflict? What caused it? What brought things to a head? Once you determine the cause, you can deal with the source rather than the symptoms. In most cases, a conflict can be resolved when both parties are willing to settle the struggle peacefully and amicably. Here are the causes of most conflicts:

In marriage—it's two selfish people wanting their own way

In business—it's two rival employees arguing over who has the better idea

In the neighborhood—it's two neighbors with different thoughts about that barking dog

In theology—it's two scholars who believe their own interpretation of Scripture is correct

In relationships—it's pride, envy, or anger that won't admit any wrongdoing

In the church—it's a power struggle between members who are arguing over how something should be done (even a matter as trivial as the color of the paint in the fellowship hall!)

In Nehemiah's case, the conflicts demanding his attention were more than superficial. They were not about simple matters such as paint color. In fact, hatred was the basis for the conflicts he was facing. And he knew he shouldn't try to deal with this on his own. As always, Nehemiah, a man of prayer, asked for God to intervene and deal with his nation's enemies.

When conflicts arise, make prayer your starting point too. Then take the next step:

Keep the conflict contained. Confine the dispute to those who can be part of the solution. If you are in conflict with another person, go to that person privately. Don't involve others if it might undermine relationships. When it comes to conflicts among believers, Jesus gave a clear, step-by-step pattern to follow:

> If your brother sins against you, go and tell him his fault between you and him alone. If he hears you, you have gained your brother. But if he will not hear, take with you one or two more, that "by the mouth of two

or three witnesses every word may be established."
And if he refuses to hear them, tell it to the church
(Matthew 18:15-17).

Find a solution to the conflict. If you enter into conflict management
with the mind-set that there are no disagreements that cannot be
resolved, you are well on your way to a solution. When people are
willing to work through the issues together, then you'll have things
moving toward a positive conclusion.

In general, people want peace, but they want it on their terms.
There isn't always a common desire for resolution. Your job as a
leader is to create an environment in which the fewest number of
people are needed to successfully work through the issues. When
you are faced with relationship issues and disagreements, you are
to act as an arbitrator, referee, and peacemaker. However, if necessary, you must also act as a judge and hand down a verdict that will
help end the conflict.

NEHEMIAH ON LEADERSHIP

Nehemiah faced incredible opposition during his two ten-
ures as governor. The strife that constantly took place around him
would have caused a lesser man to give up. But Nehemiah was not
just any man: He was God's man—a leader after God's own heart.
He was able to manage conflict through prayer, wisdom, and a
keen sense of purpose. He was able to discern the where and why
of conflict. And when it came to dealing with his enemies, he realized reconciliation was not possible because of their deep-seated
hatred for the Jews. Therefore, Nehemiah needed to trust God to
see him through.

Conflicts will come in all sizes and shapes. Fortunately for you,
yours probably won't be as severe as those Nehemiah encountered.
Obviously, like Nehemiah, prayer for wisdom is a must. And three
qualities that helped Nehemiah will help you too as you manage
your conflicts:

Character. Character is integrity under fire. Repeatedly, Nehemiah's character was challenged. And, in every case, his character was 100 percent validated. His strength of character came from his love and understanding of God's Word. He lived out the Scriptures. Nehemiah knew what many Christian leaders forget: When you neglect the study of God's Word, you lose the anchor for your character. Then, as your character drifts, you lose your ability to accurately discern and act upon the issues which confront you.

Confidence. A man's confidence is an outgrowth of his character. This is what gives you the strength to fulfill your roles and God's purposes. Nehemiah was confident of his purpose. Therefore he never doubted his mission, even under extreme fire. He never lost confidence in God's calling on his life. As a result, he was able to handle the many conflicts he faced. If you allow conflict, whether personal or corporate, to divert your focus from your responsibilities and appointed tasks, you can lose your confidence.

Courage. Courage is not the *absence* of fear. Rather, it's the *control* of fear. Nehemiah repeatedly had opportunities to collapse in defeat as a result of the many conflicts he faced. Yet he stood firm and trusted the Lord as he faced attacks, slander, and subversion.

Character, confidence, and *courage.* These are the three legs that will support your ability to manage conflict. The absence of any one of these three qualities will lessen your effectiveness. As a man after God's own heart, you'll want to cultivate these three traits. Then you will be a successful leader who can manage conflict in God's way with God's strength.

12

VISION...GIVES DIRECTION TO YOUR LEADERSHIP

I ask that you send me to Judah,
to the city of my fathers' tombs, that I may rebuild it
(NEHEMIAH 2:5).

At last—it's done! Over! Finished! All praise be to God!
As Nehemiah—who by now was haggard, exhausted, and dirty—gazed at the completed wall, his emotions soared. He wanted to celebrate. By all calculations, the impossible had been achieved. Against all odds, the people had rallied, labored, sacrificed, and accomplished the inconceivable.

I can hardly believe it! For 52 days we battled constantly against intimidation, threats, and verbal abuse. We kept up a day-and-night vigil at the wall for almost three months. I've never felt this exhausted. What many people said couldn't be done is finally done. There is much to give thanks to the Lord God for.

So now what was Nehemiah supposed to do? He could have responded in the way some people do today. He could have stopped right then and there and cashed in on his success. He could have written a bestseller entitled *How to Rebuild Your Wall*. He could have gone out on the speaking circuit and shared his success story and his approach to wall-building. He could have taken some time off for vacation at the sea, or sat around getting some rest and relaxation. After all, he deserved it, right? His body could have used some tender loving care after all he had been through. Or he could have even advertised his skills for other struggling cities that needed his expertise.

Or Nehemiah's emotional response could have swung the other direction. He could have had a massive letdown like that of a warrior who has no more wars to fight. He could have felt he no longer had a purpose, that there was no reason for him to keep moving forward. This is what happens to leaders who have myopic vision. They never look beyond their present, most pressing problem. Once the assignment is over, they feel lost until they find a new project, a different cause. But that was not the case with Nehemiah. He had bigger plans than just the rebuilding of the wall.

As we've already seen, Nehemiah was a man after God's own heart. In no way could he rest on his laurels, or succumb to any kind of letdown. His master plan called for stages and phases. And building and repairing the wall was only the beginning. He had dared to look beyond the most urgent problem, the need for a solid and completed wall. Once that problem was solved, Nehemiah praised God, celebrated with the people, and then lost no time diving into his next planned project and cause to benefit God's people. His goal was to also rebuild the city, revitalize the Jewish culture, and revive the nation's pride.

Failing to Focus on the Future

In his book *The Top Ten Mistakes Leaders Make*, Hans Finzel presents "a failure to focus on the future" as his #10 mistake leaders make. He states, "If leadership is about the future, then the worst thing a leader can do is fear the future." He continues, "Our present methods are already obsolete, so we constantly refine, improve, listen, and learn. Others may fear, but he or she who leads must boldly face the future." Then Finzel cites the following letter, which was written by a future president of the United States who wanted to put the brakes on the future of railroad expansion:

January 31, 1829

To: President Jackson

As you may well know, Mr President, "railroad" car-riages are pulled at the enormous speed of 15 miles per hour by "engines" which, in addition to endangering life and limb of passengers, roar and snort their way through the countryside, setting fire to crops, scaring the livestock and frightening women and children. The Almighty certainly never intended that people should travel at such breakneck speed.

Martin Van Buren
Governor of New York[34]

Great Leaders Have Vision

If hindsight gives you 20/20 vision, then foresight gives you lim-itless vision. Thinking about the future gives you the horizon and beyond.

Because of its potential, few things are more important for strengthening your leadership than vision. Good leaders plan for the future. They foresee that something special or better is out there. They see what others can't see. And they anticipate. Call it imag-ination, creativity, or a natural sense for the possibility of what could happen if… Whatever you want to call it, these special lead-ers, whether of a few or many, are forward thinkers. The future may be vague and undefined at the moment, but that doesn't stop these visionaries from looking ahead with anticipation.

The great leaders of the past have consistently been visionaries. Some of them were conquerors, like William the Conqueror, Alex-ander the Great, Julius Caesar, Attila the Hun, and Napoleon. Others were thinkers like Sir Isaac Newton and Albert Einstein. Still oth-ers were inventors like Thomas Edison and Alexander Graham Bell.

Then there are modern-day business visionaries like Bill Gates of Microsoft and the late Steve Jobs of Apple. All of these individuals—past and present—have one thing in common: Whether it's lands to conquer, science problems to solve, new products to invent, or improved operating systems for computers, they all had a vision!

Two Men Who Were Visionaries

Have you ever been in the minority when it came to opinions regarding your great new idea? You believe in your plan with all your heart—you are convinced that it's the right way to go. It's a can't-miss opportunity. But why is it that, because of just one tiny problem or unsettled question, no one else on the management team agrees?

Well, welcome to the Old Testament world of Joshua and Caleb. You probably remember their story…

The children of Israel had settled at the foot of Mount Sinai for a year following their exodus from Egypt. While there, Moses received the Ten Commandments and the details for constructing the tabernacle for worship. God's original intent was to bring the people into the Promised Land by a direct route, a mere 11-day journey (150 miles) from Mount Sinai to the staging area for entering their soon-to-be permanent home. While the people camped near the borders of the Promised Land, Moses asked each tribe to select a leader from among themselves to spy out the land before Israel began its invasion (Numbers 13:2).

After 40 days of sleuthing back and forth and up and down the land, the spies returned with their firsthand reports. Ten of the spies gave a report that was not good. They expressed the obvious by saying the land was lush and fertile. But then they described the people as too strong, stating that some of them were giants. They saw themselves as "grasshoppers" in comparison to these people (verse 33).

By contrast, Caleb, who dissented from the majority report, said, "Let us go up at once and take possession, for we are well able to overcome it" (verse 30). Then, as fear and frustration mounted in the hearts of the people, Joshua, the other dissenter, added this visionary endorsement: "If the LORD delights in us, then He will bring us into this land and give it to us...Only do not rebel against the LORD, nor fear the people of the land...the LORD is with us. Do not fear them" (14:8-9).

Ten men saw only giants and defeat, while two men saw victory. Ten were fearful, while two were fearless. Ten saw only failure, while two saw God's future. Tragically, because the people sided with the timid ten, the entire generation that came out of Egypt was not allowed to enter the land. Over the next 40 years in the wilderness, they died in their doubt without experiencing the blessings promised to those who believed in God's promise and power.

Joshua and Caleb, however, who were visionary and trusted God, were the leaders who experienced the Lord's victory along with that next generation. Sadly, the leaders who lacked faith influenced and doomed a whole generation to wander in the desert until their deaths.

What about you? Are you promoting faith...or fear? Are you creating doubt...or giving direction? The account about the ten spies filled with fear confirms the proverb that states, "Where there is no vision, the people perish" (Proverbs 29:18 KJV).

A Vision's Key Features

Hopefully you are realizing the importance of visionary thinking. So, with its significance in mind, here are some key features that a vision—or desired outcome—must possess:

A vision must be felt deeply. The more strongly a visionary believes in a cause, mission, or dream, the more likely he will be able to excite and involve others. If he himself isn't willing to make sacrifices, how can he expect others to make sacrifices? This was one of the key elements of Nehemiah's strength. He saw the desperate plight of the people, his soul was stirred, and he put together a plan for helping them.

A vision must be shared. A vision, if left unacted upon, is only a dream. If a leader can properly communicate his vision, it can become a powerful motivational force. A leader's passion can't merely be a slogan hanging on a wall or shouted out once in a while, or a dream in his head. If that vision is to gain form, take flight, be useful, and make a difference, it must be developed and passed on to others. Sharing an exciting vision with others in a way that compels them to act is an element of successful leadership.

A vision must inspire. A visionary must stir emotion in his listeners and inspire enthusiasm, belief, and commitment. The leader's vision is even more powerful if he can convince others of its benefits to them and to others. In the business world, employees probably understand that they are producing goods to make money for their company's owners and to pay their own salaries. But when they are given a vision of just how important these goods are to the productivity and well-being of others—even around the world—they begin to get inspired and take pride in their jobs and products. Now they understand, for instance, that their creations are saving the lives of premature babies or protecting the men and women in the military who are in harm's way! Encouraging your followers to remember the end-result benefits of their work inspires them to do well.

A good leader must challenge people to surpass themselves, to stretch and reach, to see the noble nature of each project or idea. If it's a worthy future that the visionary is proposing, that makes each employee's job that much easier and more rewarding.

A vision must unify. If the visionary is successful and has clearly set a direction and purpose for his followers, he will generate loyalty and unity through the mutual involvement of his listeners. If his leadership is in the context of a company, he will describe and reflect on the unique strengths, culture, values, beliefs, and direction that this new idea, product, concept, or vision will have on the organization. He will convince his fellow workers that their individual efforts are part of something bigger than themselves and their daily work, and that together, they can succeed in making the vision become reality.

A vision must be repeatedly shared. A visionary doesn't forget his dreams. They are permanently burned into his brain. They keep *him* up at night—they drive *him* forward. But because his people don't "own" this vision in the same way he does, he needs to repeatedly share it or the people will forget about it. So the leader must remind *them* often of their purpose, their cause, their mission, their contribution. He must do this constantly and continously. The leader must prompt his people to recall and remember the vision that's been placed before them.

Are you becoming convinced of the power of vision? When a leader believes in an idea or mission, it can become a great source of strength both for him and for others. That's what you are about to see in the life of Nehemiah—so read on!

Extended Vision

Nehemiah's mission was just beginning. His vision included much, much more than just the wall. And his vision did not stop with the building, but would also include the builders—the people. After the wall was completed, he would take off his construction hat and exchange it for a governor's administrative hat. He would proceed to fight for the people's welfare and their heritage.

Nehemiah's first objective—Phase One—had been reached: the building of the wall (Nehemiah 1–6). Nehemiah had used his visionary thinking to inspire the people to do the impossible. But there was more to come. Now read on to see more of his visionary thinking as he moved ahead with Phase Two of his master plan.

He was able to communicate his vision to others. Once again, a visionary must communicate his vision. A leader without a vision lacks direction, and a leader who doesn't communicate his vision will lack followers. From the time Nehemiah came down from inspecting the wall, he instilled a vision in people's hearts and minds. He painted a picture of the necessity for a protective wall around the city. He gave the people hope for a better future.

It's one thing to have a vision, and it's quite another to be able to communicate that vision to others in a way that will move them to embrace and internalize it for themselves. Do you recall how Nehemiah communicated his vision?

> I said to them, "You see the distress that we are in, how Jerusalem lies waste, and its gates are burned with fire. Come and let us build the wall of Jerusalem, that we may no longer be a reproach." And I told them of the hand of my God which had been good upon me, and also of the king's words that he had spoken to me (Nehemiah 2:17-18).

How effective was he in communicating that vision? "So they said, 'Let us rise up and build.' Then they set their hands to this good work" (verse 18).

He flexed as the scope of his vision changed. Phase One of Nehemiah's vision required that he initiate (get it planned), motivate (get it started), and rejuvenate (keep it going when the workers became discouraged). Upon the completion of Phase One, Nehemiah needed to transition to Phase Two of his vision. He strengthened, delegated, managed, and looked to the future.

First, Nehemiah *strengthened*. After the wall was completed, more work needed to be done: "Then it was, when the wall was built and I had hung the doors, when the gatekeepers, the singers, and the Levites had been appointed" (7:1).

Second, Nehemiah *delegated*. A wise leader knows he must find others to share the burden of leadership. And so he looked for helpers who would take on various responsibilities. If Nehemiah was to govern the region, he had to choose competent assistants. He needed helpers who were trustworthy and could lead with integrity. Here's what Nehemiah said about two of the appointments: He "gave the charge of Jerusalem to my brother Hanani, and [he assigned] Hananiah the leader of the citadel, for he was a faithful man and feared God more than many" (7:2). You'll remember that Nehemiah's brother, Hanani, was the one who brought him the initial report about conditions in Jerusalem (1:2).

Third, Nehemiah *managed.* He gave directions to his two leaders: "I said to them, 'Do not let the gates of Jerusalem be opened until the sun is hot; and while they stand guard, let them shut and bar the doors; and appoint guards from among the inhabitants of Jerusalem, one at his watch station and another in front of his own house'" (verse 3).

Fourth, Nehemiah *planned.* As you've seen throughout this chapter, a wise leader consolidates in the present, and plans for the future. "Now the city was large and spacious, but the people in it were few, and the houses were not rebuilt" (verse 4). Nehemiah's mandate for the future came from God: "My God put it into my heart to gather the nobles, the rulers, and the people, that they might be registered by genealogy" (verse 5).

What was Nehemiah thinking? He noticed that the population of Jerusalem was quite small in relation to the size of the territory enclosed within the wall. In much of the walled city, the houses had never been rebuilt. For the city to regain its prominence in the region, it needed to be vibrant, active, and populated. Nehemiah's first step was to find out who might be good candidates to return to Jerusalem and reside in the city.

He began by taking a census and registering the people (verses 6-73). In the course of doing this, his work is interrupted by a spiritual awakening (Nehemiah 8–10), which turned out to be a good thing. Why? Because God would use the revival to prepare the hearts of His people for the difficult task of relocating many families into the walled city (Nehemiah 11).

NEHEMIAH ON LEADERSHIP

To be a strong and successful leader, you must cultivate the ability to picture the end results. Whether you're dealing with family matters or business endeavors, what will be the end result of this new decision, direction, policy, or method of operating? As a responsible leader you must always try to envision how a change will affect not only present conditions but future health and growth.

Nehemiah was a leader because he perceived what nine genera-
tions had failed to see. He envisioned a walled city and its vibrant,
noble people radiating God's blessings to a watching and disbe-
lieving world.

Every strong leader has a passion for something. What are you
passionate about? What is your driving force? What keeps you
going when things get difficult?

Then answer these important questions as well: Is yours a noble
passion like Nehemiah's was? Will others benefit from your vision
both in the present and in the months and years to come?

Nehemiah inspired a whole generation with his vision. How
can you articulate and inspire others with your vision for the future?
And how can you take a vision that's in your mind and heart and
pass it along to others so they can carry it out? Here are some basic
steps that may help you turn a vision into reality:

> Step #1—Put your dreams on paper. Note the people
> they would affect and benefit. Then pray for God to
> affirm whether your dreams are His will.

> Step #2—Take time to think about the future. What
> would happen if your ideas were realized? Once you have
> your answer, go to the next step.

> Step #3—Set goals that reflect this ideal future. It's been
> said, "What your mind can conceive, it can achieve."
> Measurable goals will help you succeed in fulfilling your
> dreams.

> Step #4—Enlist the support of others. Start with God by
> making sure this is something that's within His will. Ask
> others for advice. Seek help as you develop your strat-
> egy. If it's a spiritual matter, ask others to think and pray
> along with you as you look to God for His "go ahead" and
> direction.

> Step #5—Keep moving forward. Regardless of sure-to-
> come roadblocks and opposition, keep moving forward.

Refuse to give up on what is a right direction for your family, team, cause, or company. If your idea is a good one, somehow it will take root and blossom. If it's an idea that has spiritual implications and you believe it is God's will, then take steps to act upon your vision. After all, you are only endeavoring to fulfill His desire. Remember Psalm 37:4: "Delight yourself also in the LORD, and He shall give you the desires of your heart."

The world is filled with wannabe leaders. Their impact is limited because they only *observe* the present—the here-and-now. They only *look* at the possibilities. But the real leader, the successful leader, is one who *perceives*. His perceptions makes him able to *see* the possibilities—the future. Which one are you? Are you one who simply *looks*, or do you *see* what could be?

> *Those who have most powerfully and permanently influenced their generation have been the "seers"— men who have seen more and farther than others. Men of faith, for faith is vision.*[35]

13

RENEWAL...REFRESHES YOUR LEADERSHIP

*So Ezra the priest brought the Law
before the assembly... Then he read from it...
from morning until midday*

(NEHEMIAH 8:2-3).

As Nehemiah walked toward Ezra's house in Jerusalem, he was deep in thought. Even though he hadn't had much time for reading during the building of the wall, he had still managed to scan a few of Ezra's scrolls. In them, he had read some of the history surrounding the return to Jerusalem of the 50,000 exiles under the leadership of Zerubbabel. He couldn't help but become excited as he thought about a plan that had been formulating in his mind.

At the doorway to Ezra's residence, Nehemiah took off his sandals. As was customary, a servant came and washed Nehemiah's feet. Ezra's home was modest but adequate. Manuscripts and scrolls were visible everywhere and stored in a haphazard manner. These were the telltale signs that this was the sanctuary of a scribe. Nehemiah greeted Ezra with a heartfelt "Shalom," which means "peace" and is also used to say hello or good-bye.

As the two men reclined while enjoying a Persian tea, Nehemiah ventured, "I'm sorry I haven't been able to come by and see you these past several months."

Accepting his apology, Ezra smiled and mused, "It's not as if you haven't had your hands full! Even though I'm cloistered away here trying to chronicle our people's return from exile, I would rather have been more visible and supportive." With that remark, Nehemiah knew he had his opening…

"As I was reading through your scrolls last night, I couldn't help but notice some similarities between your description of the events surrounding the celebration of the Feast of Trumpets over 90 years ago and our present time. According to your writings, the people were not just celebrating the Feast—they were also anticipating the completion of the temple. Am I not right?"

Ezra nodded.

Nehemiah went on, "So, like them, when we celebrate this new month in a few days, we too will have much to celebrate now that the wall is completed."

"Right again," said Ezra.

Now it was time for Nehemiah to bring up what he wanted to say. "Since you regretted not being more visible these past months, do you think you could pull yourself away from your writings and come celebrate the Feast of Trumpets with the people? They've worked extremely hard—heroically, actually. I know your presence would mean a lot to them. Who knows, maybe you'll get a chance to read to us from the Law. I don't know about any of the others, but I would love to hear you teach from God's Word."

Ezra nodded and smiled. Nehemiah was thrilled at the prospect of hearing the famed Ezra read from God's Law. But then Ezra brought him back to reality by broaching the problem Nehemiah had been working on for the past several days. "I have just one question. How are you going to get people to move back into Jerusalem?"

Everyone Needs Renewal

Question: How long can you drive your car? Answer: Until it runs out of gas. And how long can you run your portable DVD player? Until the batteries die.

Burnout is a term that's used to describe what happens when a leader's physical, mental, or spiritual gas tank hits empty. When that happens, he is likely to lose his momentum, direction, and energy. And he can easily become discouraged, depressed, or defeated. When that happens, how can he get back on track? What can he do to revive himself?

Renewal is the answer. By this I mean refilling the physical, mental, and spiritual gas tank, or recharging one's batteries. Unfortunately, renewal is something many leaders neglect in their own lives. But doing that can seriously have an impact on your ability to lead. Here are some thoughts that help point out the importance of frequent renewal:

Remember God ordered one day a week for renewal. God created us and knows us better than we know ourselves. That is why, early in Israel's history, God asked his people to rest one day a week from their work—He knew they would need frequent refreshment and renewal.

These thousands of years later, nothing has changed. In fact, we can probably say the pace of life continues to become more and more hectic. A day of rest does wonders for your productivity during the other six days! God knows best, and His prescription for renewal still stands: "Six days you shall do your work, and on the seventh day you shall rest, that your ox and your donkey may rest, and the son of your female servant and the stranger may be refreshed" (Exodus 23:12).

Realize renewal is vital to effective and successful leadership. Just as you keep a watchful eye on the gas gauge in your automobile, you must be careful to recognize your personal indicators that renewal is needed. Is your temper short? Your patience waning? Your excitement nil? These are symptoms that warn you it's time to act, to take care of yourself.

One leader who failed to recognize the symptoms of burnout was the prophet Elijah. You can read the full story of what happened to him in 1 Kings 18–19, but here's a brief overview of what took place:

Elijah was a courageous leader who successfully confronted 450 prophets of the false god Baal, as well as 400 prophets of Asherah, another local deity. His emotional high from this incredible encounter was soon shattered when the evil Queen Jezebel threatened to take his life. He had just finished confronting hundreds of prophets, but that had worn him out, and his emotions were not strong enough to keep him going. In discouragement and fear, he ran from Jezebel.

Elijah fell into such great despair that he went so far as to ask God to let him die. But God provided Elijah with food and rest. Then a strengthened Elijah was given a revelation of God Himself. With a renewed sense of God's control over all things and a dose of fresh energy, Elijah was recharged and ready for his next task.

Take a lesson from Elijah: Don't depend on your emotions to keep you going. They may make you a more personable leader, but they are fickle and can also cause you to turn into a poor leader who makes bad decisions.

Remember renewal means going back to the basics. Renewal involves reinventing your successful past. What were the basics that motivated and energized you when you first set out to achieve your goals? Run through the list below and see how you are doing in each area.

Physical renewal—"The world is run by tired men" is unfortunately a true statement. They are dedicated...but tired. And fatigue defeats productivity and success. This means it's important for every leader to get some rest, and even some exercise. In Nehemiah 4:10, we read that the workers in Jerusalem grew tired from building the wall. As a result, they became discouraged and defeated.

Perhaps you need to spend a few days resting or relaxing in a quiet (or quieter!) place. A change of scenery, perhaps? This is what Jesus proposed for the health of His disciples after a difficult time of nonstop ministry:

> The apostles gathered to Jesus and told Him all things,
> both what they had done and what they had taught.

And He said to them, "Come aside by yourselves to a
deserted place and rest a while." For there were many
coming and going, and they did not even have time
to eat. So they departed to a deserted place in the boat
by themselves (Mark 6:30-32).

Jesus created man. He knew that His disciples needed rest and
renewal. Even He became tired. Yet, at times, leaders and people in
the ministry feel guilty if they don't drive themselves to the point of
exhaustion. The Scottish minister Robert Murray McCheyne was
a prime example of this drive. When he lay dying at the age of 29,
he turned to a friend and said, "God gave me a message to deliver
and a horse to ride. Alas, I have killed the horse and now I cannot
deliver the message."

Isaiah 40:31 gives us insight into the connection of the spiritual
life with the physical: "Those who wait on the LORD shall renew
their strength; they shall mount up with wings like eagles, they shall
run and not be weary, they shall walk and not faint."

When believers are patient and wait on the Lord's direction,
rather than wearing out their physical and emotional energy on
issues, they can be assured of God's strength when they are confronted with trials and all kinds of decisions that must be made.
Life, ministry, work, relationships, and leadership are not sprint
races. They are marathons. Your job? Pace yourself to go the distance.

Mental renewal—This means taking some time to think. To reex-
amine your goals. When you have some time to yourself, ask, "Am
I still heading in the right direction...or have I lost sight of my
original goals and objectives? How is my attitude? Am I short-
tempered? Frayed around the edges? Is self-doubt creeping in? Is
my confidence beginning to erode? Am I getting a vague sense
that I missed an important turn somewhere along the way?" This
kind of self-examination is helpful. You may even consider taking
a refresher course in your occupational field to find out what's new
or what changes are coming in the future.

Spiritual renewal—This means going back to what energized you in the first place—the Lord. The apostle Paul was familiar with this spiritual basic: "Therefore we do not lose heart. Even though our outward man is perishing, yet the inward man is being renewed day by day" (2 Corinthians 4:16).

Have you lost sight of the most important priority in your life—Jesus? This world exerts a powerful pull even on committed Christians. Little by little it's easy to become swept up in the cares of this world.

Maybe it's time for a spiritual revival, for getting back to the basics which have possibly been neglected—prayer, Bible reading, fellowship, and worship. And don't forget repentance. Follow this wise advice for physical, mental, and spiritual renewal:

> Lay aside every weight, and the sin which so easily ensnares us, and let us run with endurance the race that is set before us, looking unto Jesus, the author and finisher of our faith (Hebrews 12:1-2).

Realize change is a form of renewal. What happens when you get bogged down in a problem? Besides getting depressed, you can become mentally sluggish, physically drained, and often emotionally strung out. You don't have time to take a vacation, or take a nap. This is only Monday, so weekend rest is not an option. How do you break out of your demanding routine? You can simply make a change. Any change. Winston Churchill stated, "Change is as good as rest." So...take a break. Stretch. Go for a walk. Or simply switch tasks for a while. Do something different until you experience a renewed enthusiasm for once again tackling whatever it is that has bogged you down.

Rejoice! Renewal is an opportunity to reinvent yourself. No one is ever completely where they want to be physically, mentally, emotionally, and especially spiritually. That's the bad news. But the good news is that you can get up each day and fix that. You can be a different you, a better you, a more loving you, a more disciplined you, etc., tomorrow.

The choice is yours. You can renew your body by taking a short jog or walk. You can renew your mind by reading a book or newspaper. You can renew your spiritual life by reading your Bible and talking things over with God. These are choices you can make if you truly want renewal in your life. Otherwise, go on living and being the less-than-your-best you. Ask yourself, Do I really want to keep on living like this? Probably no! Well then, do something about it!

Here's an energizing thought from the Bible: God offers you a fresh infusion of His mercy and strength every morning. Start each day with this encouragement: "Through the LORD's mercies we are not consumed, because His compassions fail not. They are new every morning; great is Your faithfulness" (Lamentations 3:22-23).

Setting the Scene

Now let's go back to the opening scene of this chapter to God's scribe, Ezra. Ezra is now introduced into our portrait of a leader after God's own heart. Soon (in Nehemiah chapter 8) Ezra will begin reading and explaining God's Word to his audience. The people of Jerusalem, who have labored hard to build and complete the wall, have just come through a horrendous period of physical and emotional stress. Probably little energy was left in their heart, soul, and strength at this point. Renewal of the heart and mind was desperately needed.

While Nehemiah was the governor and in many ways a spiritual leader, and even at times a teacher, he knew he was not a specialist in teaching God's Word. He was a layman. He was just like the people he was leading. So here we witness yet another dimension of his leadership. Here we see his willingness to share his leadership role with others. Earlier, he had turned to his brother Hanani as well as to Hananiah, who was faithful and feared the Lord (verse 2). And now he lets Ezra take the lead.

There's no doubt Nehemiah was a true man of God—a man after God's own heart. But as we step into Nehemiah chapters 8 and 9, we see him voluntarily stepping aside, taking a seat in the pew, and allowing Ezra, a priest-scribe and skilled teacher, to lead the people *and him* in spiritual renewal.

Renewal and the Word of God

Here's how spiritual renewal began for the weary wall-builders:

In God's divine timing, the date was one week after the wall was completed. It was also the first day of a new month, Tishri. And amazingly, it was also the time of the annual celebration of the Feast of Trumpets. This holy convocation for the blowing of trumpets was convened at "the Water Gate" (8:1). Through this gate, water was brought into the spacious temple area, where large numbers of people could gather.

The next few verses of Nehemiah 8 describe for us a revival in action. As you read, ask yourself, *Do I need to experience spiritual revival?* Here's how it worked in the lives of the people in that open square by the water gate. Here's the evidence that spiritual renewal was on its way:

- There was an interest in God's Word—The people asked for the reading of God's Word (verse 1).

- There was a gifted teacher—Ezra had been actively involved in teaching for the past 15 years. Upon seeing him, the people asked Ezra to bring out God's scrolls to teach them (verses 1-2).

- There was a willingness to listen to God's Word—Those who could understand were eager to listen. This teaching went on for three to five hours, "morning until midday" (verse 3).

- There was a desire to know God's Word—The people not only wanted to hear the Word, they also wanted to understand it. Thirteen other men and unnamed Levites assisted Ezra in reading and interpreting the truth. Their objective was to help their hearers to understand the relevancy of what was being read and how it applied to their lives (verses 4-8).

- There was a reverence for God's Word—"They bowed

their heads and worshiped the LORD with their faces to the ground" (verse 6).

- There was a response to God's Word—When the people heard and understood God's law, they responded with remorse over their sin (verse 9).

- There was a resolve to obey God's Word—"They found written in the Law, which the LORD had commanded by Moses, that the children of Israel should dwell in booths during the feast of the seventh month...Then the people went out...and made themselves booths" (verses 14,16).

- There was a commitment to fan the flames of renewal— This spirit of renewal wasn't just a fleeting emotion. Rather it continued on throughout the month, with further demonstrations of mourning (fasting, sackcloth, and dust) and worship and confession. The people reestablished their commitments to God and His laws (Nehemiah 9).

If you want to experience renewal, you must eagerly receive God's Word and allow His Spirit to energize you through His truths. In fact, God's Word is the epicenter of renewal. That's what Paul told the Christians in Rome: "Do not be conformed to this world, but be transformed by the renewing of your mind, that you may prove what is that good and acceptable and perfect will of God" (Romans 12:2).

Take a look at your own spiritual life. Are there any signs of spiritual renewal taking place? Obviously a man—and a leader—after God's own heart recognizes that renewal is a vital element in strong leadership. How can you fan the flames of renewal in your life? Follow the example of Nehemiah and the people of his day, and look to God's Word to refresh and renew you.

NEHEMIAH ON LEADERSHIP

A strong leader is able to distinguish the means from the end.

Building the wall was an initial but vital short-range goal. Nehemiah, however, never lost sight of the whole picture. He knew the wall would provide the people a safe environment (the means) for revival and renewal that would result in eternal rewards (the end).

To make sure this would happen, Nehemiah unselfishly stepped aside and allowed another more suitable person to lead in the renewal process. He let Ezra do his job. Nehemiah could then stand with the people and apply to his own life the same truths that they were hearing proclaimed. Spiritual renewal would bring strength to both the people and to Nehemiah the leader.

How about you? Are you seeing the need for renewal? Renewal does not happen in a singular moment. By necessity it is an ongoing process. Why? Because life and leadership are demanding. Leadership is draining, no matter who you lead or how many. It's about giving to others. And it's a constantly changing reality. Today is not yesterday, nor is it tomorrow. As a Greek philosopher said, "It is not possible to step twice into the same river."

Like that ever-moving river, the demands on your life go on. At this very moment, you are not the same person you were yesterday, last week, or last year. And neither is your group, team, family, company, or those around you, including those above you. Everything— and everyone—is in flux. To keep from being swept away by the tides of change, and to ensure the strength of your leadership, you must change—you must adapt to meet the demands of the present as well as the future. You must renew yourself physically, mentally, and especially spiritually to be equipped for life as you face it today… and then wake up tomorrow and do it all over again.

*Effective leaders allow God to shape them
into the kind of people they need to be for each
situation they encounter: They don't get stuck
on one method or mode of operation.*[36]

14

LOYALTY...AFFIRMS YOUR LEADERSHIP

During all this I was not in Jerusalem,
for in the thirty-second year of Artaxerxes
king of Babylon I had returned to the king
(NEHEMIAH 13:6).

The supplies had been purchased and were being loaded onto the camels. Nehemiah's military escort had been briefed as to the route back to Susa. For some of the soldiers, Jerusalem had become almost like home. They had become pretty settled after living in the same place for a dozen years. Others were anxious to return to family and their own culture.

For Nehemiah this was a bittersweet departure. He had come as a stranger and was now leaving as a hero—and a friend—of the people. He was leaving behind many friends and loyal supporters. It had not always been this way. Upon his arrival 12 years earlier, he had only the king's authority and a God-given passion for a successful completion of his mission. But as the people saw his commitment, his steadfast resolve even under extreme duress, and his faithful and consistent interest in their welfare, he had slowly won their allegiance.

As Nehemiah climbed into his saddle, his close friends wiped their eyes as they waved good-bye. This same heartfelt response was repeated by many others as he led the caravan through the streets of Jerusalem. The people wept and waved as he departed. But duty called. Nehemiah, ever the loyal subject, must fulfill his promise and return to the king.

Loyalty Begins with Trust

Loyalty expresses commitment, steadfastness, and faithfulness. A person can be loyal to a country, a creed, or another person, and that loyalty is nurtured in trust. If that person believes in his country and its ideal, the country receives his loyalty. If he believes in a creed, then he becomes a loyal follower. The same is true of loyalty toward an individual, or in our case, a leader—Nehemiah. If the individual believes he can trust his leader to lead him adequately, then he will be loyal.

Now everyone has loyalties. Someone or something receives their allegiance. They have put their trust in someone or something. Since that's the case, why shouldn't one's loyalty start with God? Who better to trust than Him?

You can be loyal to God because...

You can trust in God's character—What God promises, He will fulfill and provide. He is "God, who cannot lie" (Titus 1:2). There are thousands of promises in the Bible, and as King Solomon acknowledged, "Blessed be the LORD...there has not failed one word of all His good promise" (1 Kings 8:56). Because God is loyal to His promises, you can trust Him to keep them! As the apostle Paul testified, "All the promises of God in Him are Yes, and in Him Amen, to the glory of God" (2 Corinthians 1:20).

You can trust in God's presence—Because God is Spirit and cannot be seen, it is sometimes difficult to trust that He will be there for you—that He will come through on His promises. Earlier in this book we saw Joshua's example as a leader who benefited from repeated assurances of God's presence. At the time God spoke to Joshua, the latter had just become the new leader of Israel. He had taken Moses' place. So, as you might well expect, he was a bit nervous. His first assignment was to invade a well-populated, well-armed, well-defended land (Joshua 1:2). But not to worry! Why? God said, "Do not tremble or be dismayed, for the LORD your God is with you wherever you go" (verse 9). God promised to go with Joshua into the battle.

The fact of God's constant presence should be a source of comfort and strength to you. What greater support do you need than knowing that God is with you as you fight your battles? And here's the good news: The promise of God's presence still applies today, thousands of years after Joshua's day. Jesus, God in flesh, gave us the same kind of assurance: "Go therefore and make disciples of all the nations...and lo, I am with you always, even to the end of the age" (Matthew 28:19-20).

You can trust in God's answers to prayer—Again, Jesus, who is God and who cannot lie, teaches you to "ask, and it will be given to you; seek, and you will find; knock, and it will be opened to you. For everyone who asks receives, and he who seeks finds, and to him who knocks it will be opened" (Matthew 7:7-8).

And to make this trust even more complete, sometimes God answers when we don't even know how to pray about a certain issue. When that happens, the Holy Spirit steps in and prays for us, intercedes for us (Romans 8:26).

Does knowing that God hears and responds to your prayers help you to trust Him with even the smallest issues you face? It should. But how about being able to trust Him with the most important thing you possess—such as your eternal destiny? Read on.

You can trust in God's offer of eternal life—Have you ever wondered why Jesus, God in flesh, came to earth? Well, He came to die for your sins, and to offer life—abundant life, eternal life. Jesus said, "I have come that they may have life, and that they may have it more abundantly" (John 10:10). He also proclaimed, "I give them eternal life, and they shall never perish; neither shall anyone snatch them out of My hand" (John 10:28).

When you put your faith and trust in God the Son, He promises you life everlasting. Are you trusting Him now? If not, what's holding you back?

So, knowing that you can trust God for anything and everything—including your eternal destiny—should prompt your loyalty to Him, right?

Loyalty Promotes Loyalty

When it comes to followers responding to your leadership, realize that loyalty is not a response that just happens. Loyalty must be earned. And it goes both ways. As you've already read, a loyal leader expresses commitment, steadfastness, and faithfulness to those who serve him. Loyalty says, "You have been faithful to me, therefore I will be faithful to you. Your loyalty to me will be repaid with my loyalty to you."

A good leader demonstrates loyalty both at home and at work as he regards the welfare of others more highly than his own comfort and prestige. He is concerned for their problems, difficulties, and misfortunes. The welfare of others is his primary concern. People do want to be led, but they also want a leader who shows he has their best interests in mind.

This concern for others must be genuine, the real thing. If you show a false and momentary loyalty merely for the sake of gaining trust and a following, your true motives will be exposed sooner or later, and your followers will lose their incentive to remain loyal. By contrast, those who know their leader truly does care for their welfare are usually willing to follow him to the ends of the earth… and back!

Here are three instances in which loyalty promoted loyalty:

David, the shepherd boy. After David killed the giant Goliath, King Saul brought David into the palace, where he became close friends with Jonathan, Saul's oldest son. A strong bond of loyalty developed between these two young men. However, King Saul became jealous of David's fame and suspected the young man was trying to take over his throne. Jonathan remained loyal to David and defended his pure intentions to his father. Finally, in a fit of jealous rage, the king confided in Jonathan of his desire to kill David. Jonathan, in turn, warned David to flee. Just before David ran for his life, the two friends met one last time and affirmed their lifelong loyalty to each other, and Jonathan asked David to care for his family should anything happen to him. Later, after Jonathan's death, David honored Jonathan's request by caring for one of his sons (2 Samuel 4:4; 9:3).

David, the warrior. After David fled from Saul, he hid in a cave in the wilderness. While he was there, large numbers of strong men of renown came to join him as warriors. So fully did he capture their affection and allegiance that even a whispered wish was translated in their hearts as a command.

On one occasion the Philistines were encamped in the valley of Rephaim near Jerusalem and occupied David's hometown of Bethlehem. David expressed how much he wished for a drink of water from the well at Bethlehem. Well, unintended by David, his wish became his soldiers' command! Three of his loyal friends broke through the enemy lines and risked their lives to bring him a flask of water from the well.

And note this: Because David's men had risked so much to demonstrate their loyalty, he regarded the water as too sacred to drink selfishly. He then poured it out before God and his men as an act of worship (2 Samuel 23:15-16). It was actions like these that endeared David to his men, and the men to David. They were willing to die for him because they knew he would die for them.

Hudson Taylor, the missionary. Hudson Taylor was a pioneer in modern missions. He was the founder of China Inland Mission, which, over several decades, sent hundreds of missionaries to Asian countries. In an address that presented some of the secrets of Hudson Taylor's remarkably successful leadership, his successor, D.E. Hoste, had this to say about Taylor's concerns for others:

> Another secret of his influence among us lay in his
> great sympathy and thoughtful consideration for the

welfare and comfort of those about him…He mani-
fested great tenderness and patience toward the fail-
ures and shortcomings of his brethren, and was thus
able in many cases to help them reach a higher plane
of devotion.[37]

Could your family, friends, followers, fellow workers, and
employees make the same claims about you? Do you help them
reach a "higher plane"? Hopefully so!

Leaders and Loyalty

Loyalty is not servitude; it is servanthood. It flows both upward
toward superiors and downward toward followers. It is one of the
most essential qualities that a leader must first possess himself and
then instill in his followers. That's why men like David, Hudson
Taylor, and, of course, Nehemiah are such excellent role models. A
leader who possesses his own standard of loyalty will instill that
same standard in his followers. Here's what loyalty should look like:

Loyalty to God—A leader who wants to inspire others to follow after
God's own heart must first desire to fully follow God's heart himself. He must first be loyal to his God. And prayer is a primary way
to show that loyalty. A leader who doesn't pray is actually declaring his loyalty to his *own* wisdom. But a leader who prays is admit-
ting his own weaknesses and declaring his dependence and reliance
upon an all-knowing, all-wise God—a God he can trust for help in
dealing with his personal and leadership challenges.

Nehemiah, a leader after God's own heart, most definitely demonstrated his loyalty to God through his continuous commitment
to prayer.

Loyalty to God's Word—How is loyalty to God demonstrated? In
one word: obedience. That is, obedience to God's standards as communicated in the Bible. Jesus said, "If you love Me [if you are loyal
to Me], keep My commandments" (John 14:15). Loyalty involves

faithfulness to God's Word. Nehemiah endeavored to obey God's Word, whether it involved observing the Sabbath, following God's commands on interest payments, keeping the Hebrew lineage free from foreign marriages, preserving the sanctity of the temple, or making sure the prescribed holidays were properly observed. Nehemiah refused to compromise or deviate from his commitment to fulfilling God's laws.

Loyalty to your superiors—Everyone answers to someone. Even bosses have bosses. And the Bible states very clearly,

> Bondservants, be obedient to those who are your masters according to the flesh, with fear and trembling, in sincerity of heart, as to Christ; not with eyeservice, as men-pleasers, but as bondservants of Christ, doing the will of God from the heart, with goodwill doing service, as to the LORD, and not to men, knowing that whatever good anyone does, he will receive the same from the LORD, whether he is a slave or free (Ephesians 6:5-8).

Nehemiah was a loyal employee. He had asked to be relieved of his position as cupbearer for a certain length of time or until the situation in Jerusalem was stable. Whatever the arrangement, he was gone for 12 years. And evidently the king was loyal to Nehemiah—he provided Nehemiah with help and resources. Nehemiah, in turn, repaid that loyalty by returning to the king as agreed upon earlier.

Loyalty to your work—The Bible tells you exactly how you are to view your work: "Whatever you do, do it heartily, as to the Lord and not to men" (Colossians 3:23).

Nehemiah was a faithful employee. His rise to the position of cupbearer proved his allegiance and commitment to the king. He was so faithful that the king trusted Nehemiah with his very life. Therefore, when Nehemiah made the request to go to Jerusalem, the king didn't hesitate to give a positive response.

Loyalty to your workers—The Bible has much to say about the relationship between masters and servants. In all cases, bosses are told to be fair and treat their workers with respect. Here's how the apostle Paul spells out loyalty as he speaks to both employees and employers: "with goodwill [do] service, as to the Lord, and not to men, knowing that whatever good anyone does, he will receive the same from the Lord, whether he is a slave or free. And you, masters, do the same things to them, giving up threatening, knowing that your own Master also is in heaven, and there is no partiality with Him" (Ephesians 6:7-9).

Nehemiah constantly cared about the welfare of the people. Whether it was their protection from the enemy soldiers or the greedy nobles, Nehemiah stood shoulder to shoulder with the people. He sympathized with their problems (4:10-12; 5:1-5). He was willing to stop to lend an understanding ear to the difficulties they were facing. And he was willing to provide a shoulder to cry on. The workers and their families knew they could trust Nehemiah with their lives, and to show their loyalty, they did the impossible in only 52 days!

Loyal to the end—People can be fickle when it comes to loyalty. After all, loyalty requires commitment, which is based on trust...which can be fragile at best. However, our loyalty to God should never fluctuate. And a leader's loyalty to his boss, his job, his workers, his family, or whoever should be rock solid—it should be unfaltering and unfailing. If he fails to be loyal, he will fail as a leader.

Nehemiah was loyal to the end in every area of his leadership to the people and his service to the king. To the very end his constant concern was to please God. "Remember me, O my God, for good!" (13:31), he said.

Inspiring Loyalty

Clearly, loyalty is a powerful force in leadership. So what does it take to generate this kind of loyalty in those you lead? Once again, as stated earlier, loyalty starts with you, the leader. You need to remain loyal to both your ideals and the needs of your followers. Loyalty must be given downward before it can or will be given upward. Here are a few ways you can inspire loyalty in your followers:

Be loyal to your boss. Everyone answers to someone. Whoever that someone is in your sphere, be loyal. Be as faithful to that person as you would be to your Lord (Ephesians 6:5). This loyalty will provide a model of loyalty to those you lead.

Be impartial. Showing favoritism to a few is a sure way to create distrust among others. If a person's promotion is based on being in the "good old boys' club" rather than on competence, then don't expect loyalty from your workers. Likewise, when it comes to reprimands, be like Nehemiah: Don't play favorites (Nehemiah 5:7). He showed no respect for a person's office or rank. The nobles and spiritual rulers all received his displeasure equally.

Be consistent. Remember that loyalty is based on trust. If you are erratic or irrational in your decisions and actions, people won't be able to trust you as a leader. Consistency is vital.

Be faithful. If you say you are going to do something, make sure you follow through. If you make a promise, take it seriously and don't forget it. In the eyes of your people, a forgotten promise is a broken promise. It says they—and your promise—aren't that important to you. They then reason that if *they* aren't important to you, then whatever it is they're *doing* for you isn't that important either.

Be honest. The Bible speaks clearly and repeatedly about honesty. We may reason to ourselves that it's okay to tell a little "white lie" or a half-truth or to omit a vital detail or piece of information. But as the saying goes, "Your sins will find you out." And once you are caught in a lie by those closest to you—your family, your acquaintances, or your workers—they will have a difficult time ever trusting you again. Besides the fact telling a lie is a sin, no lie is worth risking the loyalty of your people.

Be decisive. As Matthew 5:37 says, "Let your 'Yes' be 'Yes' and your 'No,' 'No.'" Indecision is worse than no decision—or even the wrong decision. "He who hesitates is lost" is a saying that speaks as much about garnering loyalty as it does about failure. Seek answers and solutions, and above all, seek God's will. And once you have determined the direction you will take, be decisive and go into immediate action. Don't waver or hesitate.

Be real. If you as a leader are in over your head and you try to bluff your way through your situation, your people will see right through your facade. A real leader will admit to his shortcomings and seek the aid of others. Your people want to see you succeed as much as you do, so let them help by being open to advice.

Be a servant. Nehemiah consistently showed a servant's heart. He put others first. He showed a concern for the welfare of others (2:10). This concern found expression in his prayers, fasting, and tears, and ultimately it translated into his willingness to travel thousands of miles to Jerusalem to serve an impoverished and discouraged community. Nehemiah was not pretentious in his role as governor. And he did not abuse his authority. In fact, he used his position as a platform to serve the people, constantly putting others ahead of his own agenda. His example lived out the principle taught by the greatest servant of all and the greatest leader of all, Jesus Christ:

> Whoever desires to become great among you, let him be your servant. And whoever desires to be first among you, let him be your slave—just as the Son of Man did not come to be served, but to serve (Matthew 20:26-28).

NEHEMIAH ON LEADERSHIP

How do you determine if a leader is successful? Is it the size of his organization or army? Is it the size of his company's revenues? True, profit margin is a measure of success, and the larger an organization or army is, the more likely it is people will conclude you're a good leader. But size or numbers can be deceptive. Many generals with massive armies have been defeated by much smaller forces, and most smaller companies can produce higher profit margins than the corporate giants.

So what might be a better indicator of success for a leader? In a word, loyalty. The greatest leaders throughout history have produced the greatest level of loyalty in their followers. With loyal devotion, they can and have produced the greatest of results. Here are but a few examples:

Leonidas, the king of Sparta, with a personal bodyguard of 300 men—the most elite of the Spartan forces—along with additional forces that brought his numbers to some 7000 Greek soldiers, defended the narrow mountain pass of Thermopylae against the massive Persian army of King Xerxes—an army estimated to number between 100,000 to 200,000 strong. During the battle Leonidas sent away some of his troops, and his loyal 300 Spartans and some others remained. When Leonidas fell in the battle, his loyal men surrounded his body and refused to retreat. They were all killed by the Persians. Without the help of Leonidas and his 300 devoted Spartan soldiers, who defied the tyranny of Xerxes at Thermopylae, the Greek city-states of that day would have been overrun by the Persian hordes.

Robert E. Lee, general of the Confederate army during the US Civil War, repeatedly defended his beloved state of Virginia and outmaneuvered massive Union armies who came up against him. (The Union generals nicknamed him Gray Fox because of his many successes.) Lee's effectiveness was due partly to his battle strategies, but more significantly it was possible because of the exceptional loyalty and trust he had gained from his men.

Jesus, the greatest leader of all time, returned to heaven leaving behind 120 followers, both men and women, most of whom were just ordinary people with little or no money, influence, or education.

But because of their unswerving loyalty to their Savior, they were willing to suffer the ultimate sacrifice of death to spread the gospel. They were responding to Jesus' demonstration of loyalty toward them—which applies to us as well: "When we were still without strength, in due time Christ died for the ungodly" (Romans 5:6). Two thousand years later that loyalty continues on in the lives of countless millions around the world. It is a loyalty that has never faded or been extinguished, a loyalty that will last for all eternity.

Nehemiah was just a civil servant. He was not a Spartan king. He was not a military general. But he accomplished what no other person had been able to do. Even after 90 years had passed and thousands of Jews had returned to Judah, the wall around Jerusalem was still in ruins. The people were discouraged and defeated. But Nehemiah's loyalty to his God, to his king, and then to the people resulted in a loyal response not only from God, but also from the king he served as well as the people who did the work! Nehemiah was a leader after God's own heart, and loyalty marked and affirmed his leadership.

The first thing a young officer must do when he joins
the Army is to fight a battle, and that battle is for the
hearts of his men. If he wins that battle and subsequent
similar ones, his men will follow him anywhere;
if he loses it, he will never do any real good.[38]

—VISCOUNT MONTGOMERY OF ALAMEIN,
FIELD MARSHAL, 8TH ARMY, WWII

15

INTEGRITY...VALIDATES YOUR LEADERSHIP

From the time that I was appointed to be their governor...
twelve years, neither I nor my brothers
ate the governor's provisions...
I did not demand the governor's provisions,
because the bondage was heavy on this people
(NEHEMIAH 5:14,18).

As Nehemiah paced back and forth in his quarters, he reviewed, in his mind, the events of the past 12 years. He had replayed these events over and over in his mind more times than he could count. There had been many magnificent successes, all praise be to the Lord God! Of course there was the wall, probably the most visible accomplishment. And as he prepared to dictate more details about that project to his scribe, he suddenly remembered an event that almost brought the building project crashing down.

Not a very good memory, to be sure, he muttered. Unfortunately, it involved the despicable actions of the nobles and rulers.

How to begin? Nehemiah wondered. *Ah, yes!* And thus he stated, "There was a great outcry of the people and their wives against their Jewish brethren" (Nehemiah 5:1). He then raced through the sad tale of the rich taking advantage of the poor people of Judea by charging excessive interest. When Nehemiah finished telling how the incident had been resolved successfully, he then thought about who might be reading this account. *Oh my—what if someone might think I too had somehow been involved? That I too had taken advantage of the people?*

Not wanting to blow his own trumpet, but definitely wanting to set the record straight, Nehemiah decided to give an account of his own actions then and throughout his years as governor. As he continued dictating, he prayed, and tried his best to evaluate his conduct and make sure it had been acceptable to God.

Integrity Makes a Difference

In 1517, a 34-year-old German priest named Martin Luther became outraged that people were being taught that freedom from God's punishment of sin could be purchased with money. These "indulgences" were outlined in an edict from Pope Leo X. Luther confronted the indulgence salesman, Johann Tetzel, with 95 statements, which he nailed on the door of Wittenberg Church, criticizing the Pope and explaining that the sale of these "get out of hell free passes" to be biblically incorrect.

On April 18, 1521, Luther, knowing full well the serious nature of his summons, appeared as ordered before the Diet of Worms, a general assembly of the Catholic Church in the town of Worms in Germany. He was presented with copies of his writings, which were laid out on a table. Then he was asked if the books were his, and whether or not he stood by their contents. Luther confirmed he was their author. Then he requested time to think about the answer to the second question. He prayed, consulted friends, and gave this response the next day:

> Unless I am convinced by the testimony of the Scriptures or by clear reason (for I do not trust either in the pope or in councils alone, since it is well known that they have often erred and contradicted themselves), I am bound by the Scriptures I have quoted and my conscience is captive to the Word of God. I cannot and will not retract anything, since it is neither safe nor right to go against conscience. May God help me. Amen.

Martin Luther is also quoted as saying, "Here I stand. I can do no other." But regardless of the full extent of his statement, the now-famous Ninety-Five Theses had a huge impact. Luther's integrity—his willingness to stand true to his beliefs—was a key spark that contributed to the igniting of the great Protestant Reformation.

Integrity: Don't Leave Home Without It!

What values do you admire in your superiors? That's the question two researchers asked as they conducted thousands of surveys around the world and performed more than 400 written case studies. Researchers Kouzes and Posner identified three characteristics that were most desired in a leader. Integrity was at the top of the list, followed by competence and leadership.[39]

After reading about Martin Luther and his stand for the truth, and then seeing the research done by Kouzes and Posner, it goes without saying (but I'll say it anyway) that integrity isn't something you want to leave behind when you put on your leadership hat and face your people. Because that trait is so essential, let's make sure we have a clear understanding of what it is.

The Meaning of Integrity

When used of a ship's hull, *integrity* is what makes it seaworthy. When used of a plane's wings, *integrity* is what will ensure a safe flight. When used of a chemical compound, *integrity* ensures the correctness of the formulating process. So, whether the term is used in reference to a boat, a plane, or a chemical, *integrity* ensures that the object or substance can be trusted to fulfill its intended purpose.

When applied to a person, *integrity* means being truthful, trustworthy, having convictions. It is steadfast adherence to a strict moral or ethical code. It is unimpaired in its focus. It is whole and undivided in its certainty. Integrity is what you want for yourself and for those you lead and work with. A person with integrity can be trusted. He will do the right thing for the right reason even when no one is watching.

The fact so many people lack integrity is one of the reasons this character quality is admired in a leader. When people are called to go into battle or into a business venture or into an unknown future, they want to follow someone who they can trust will do right by them. After all, their life or financial security could be at stake. And they know that a leader with integrity will keep his promises and follow through on his commitments to them.

The Nature of Integrity

Now that we know what integrity is—that it's about trustworthiness—let's see what it does.

Integrity enforces moral convictions. Integrity gives resolve to a person's actions. It is unmoved by any immorality surrounding it. A person who displays integrity will choose honesty over deceit, fairness over injustice, and a willingness to abide by rules and regulations even when those rules are disregarded by others around them. When you are searching for a problem solver, look for a person with integrity. That person will be a straight shooter, one who walks in integrity and in the truth.

Integrity protects itself. Integrity knows that its standards have been hard fought—and won. It also knows that it takes only one indiscretion to completely wipe out a long track record of integrity. One wrong action can forfeit years of trust. Therefore, it establishes a hedge of accountability for its protection.

You—and every leader—have areas of weakness. If it so happens you can't think of one or two areas where your armor is a little thin, just ask the devil. He would be glad to explore those areas for you. If you don't believe this, then you have probably just discovered one of your weaknesses.

A strong leader will purposely surround himself with accountability and safeguards not only for himself, but also for those he leads. These protective measures can help ensure against character failure and keep one's integrity intact.

When it comes to developing accountability, here are the essential elements:

- Accountability comes first from the ultimate source of accountability, God's Word. If a leader is faithful to read and study the Bible, then God, via the Holy Spirit, will expose areas of needed change. God reveals "them to us through His Spirit. For the Spirit searches all things, yes, the deep things of God" (1 Corinthians 2:10).

- Accountability comes in the form of mentors or peers. You must give these people permission to ask if you are veering off course. "As iron sharpens iron, so a man sharpens the countenance of his friend" (Proverbs 27:17).

- Accountability requires that you have a teachable spirit. Many leaders, unfortunately, ignore the cautions and concerns of their staff and associates. "Give instruction to a wise man, and he will be still wiser; Teach a just man, and he will increase in learning" (Proverbs 9:9).

Integrity creates a value system. The world has become one big "gray area," which means when it comes to right and wrong, everything has become more and more relative. Many of today's leaders take comfort in what's known as "situational ethics." That is, the situation determines their ethic, or their response. Actions and conduct are often based on the present climate of the culture. A person who follows this ethic asks, "Is my behavior acceptable to my surroundings?" But a person who is driven by integrity will ask, "Is my behavior consistent with my set of values regarding right and wrong, which are fixed and immovable and will never change?"

When it comes to integrity, something is either right or wrong, good or bad. In the secular world, a leader can't always impose his own personal standards on others, especially if they have so-called "religious" overtones. However, God has called all Christians—and this includes leaders—to live out their belief system within the world they live in. They are to abide by God's standards for holiness and truth. Though a Christian leader may not be able to expect non-Christian followers to adhere to Christian beliefs and morals, still, he can provide a work environment that operates on fair, moral, and consistent ethical standards.

However, when working within a spiritual context, a Christian leader can—and should—impose his ethical standards on those he leads, because they should share the same biblical standards in their own lives.

Integrity makes the more difficult decisions. Integrity takes courage. It chooses the higher moral ground. It understands the consequences of wrong decisions, and therefore agonizes over the decisions that must be made. Compromise, on the other hand, is easy. It takes little or no thought to choose to conform to a low standard. Any weak or unprincipled person can take the easy way out.

A strong leader, however, adopts a noble code of ethics. For you, a Christian leader, that code is the Bible. Even though people may resist your code, they will admire your focus and your tenacity to upholding that standard.

Integrity resists pride. One of the occupational hazards of leadership is pride, especially if you are doing a good job of leading and others are noticing your work and are appreciative of it. This kind of attention and accolades can lead you to think more highly of yourself than you should—that is, become prideful! And pride is selfish, while integrity is selfless. And beware: Pride is a sin whose victim is the person least aware of his problem. In fact, pride is such a serious problem that this is God's attitude toward it: "Everyone proud in heart is an abomination to the Lord" (Proverbs 16:5).

Integrity draws people to a higher standard. People function better when they are part of something that is anchored in established rules. This structure lets them know where they stand at all times. Integrity, by its very nature, pulls a person toward this structure—toward a higher standard. It promotes a higher level of behavior. It offers a better way of life. A leader with integrity can model and direct people toward this better way of living.

People in the Bible Who Model Integrity

We'll look at integrity in Nehemiah in a bit. But first let's see how integrity was described in three great biblical leaders—Samuel and Daniel in the Old Testament, and the apostle Paul in the New Testament.

Samuel—This priest who worked in the temple is one of the Bible's greatest models of integrity. From his earliest years he devoted himself to serving God's people. It wasn't easy—after all, he grew up in the temple under the care of Eli, the high priest. This means Samuel witnessed the corrupt conduct of Eli's two sons, Hophni and Phinehas. They were immoral. They didn't respect God or the people's sacrifices. Bottom line: They had no integrity, and Samuel was exposed to their flagrant lack of integrity.

Yet in spite of these negative examples, Samuel became a leader with integrity, a leader after God's own heart. As the end of his exemplary life drew near, he stood before the people one last time and challenged them to validate his conduct. Samuel had served the developing nation of Israel as a prophet, priest, and judge. He was at the end of his public career. All through it he had fought against the use of power to exploit others for private gain. For Samuel, being a leader was a stewardship.

In his final speech before the people, Samuel reminded them of his behavior. Hear his integrity:

> "I have walked before you from my childhood to this day. Here I am. Witness against me before the LORD and before His anointed: Whose ox have I taken, or whose donkey have I taken, or whom have I cheated? Whom have I oppressed, or from whose hand have I received any bribe with which to blind my eyes? I will restore it to you."…Then he said to them, "The

LORD is witness against you, and His anointed is witness this day, that you have not found anything in my
hand" (1 Samuel 12:2-3,5).

In verse 4 we see the people give their validation of his leadership
as they affirm his conduct: "You have not cheated us or oppressed us,
nor have you taken anything from any man's hand" (verse 4). Then
in verse 5 they add God to their list of witnesses: "He is witness."

Samuel's integrity was based on his desire to honor God and
serve His people. His honesty and personal integrity permeated
every area of his life. His integrity determined how he handled his
possessions, his dealings with the people, and how he treated the
weak and needy. He held himself accountable to those around him.
Because of his integrity, he was willing to open himself to the scrutiny of others, and especially to God.

Samuel's example calls us to do the same. In everything you
do as a leader, whether at home, at church, or in the workplace, let
your desire for personal integrity shine forth in what you do each
and every day. As long as you stay committed to pursuing personal
integrity, you'll be a leader others will gladly follow!

Daniel—This prophet is another great role model of integrity. Success has its rewards, but also its dangers. Because Daniel was so
good at what he did (a positive!), other leaders were envious of his
achievements (a definite negative!). The Bible assesses his abilities
in this way: "Then this Daniel distinguished himself above the governors and satraps, because an excellent spirit was in him; and the
king gave thought to setting him over the whole realm" (Daniel 6:3).

What was the response of Daniel's fellow administrators? "The
governors and satraps sought to find some charge against Daniel
concerning the kingdom" (verse 4).

What evil skeletons did they find in Daniel's closet? Because
Daniel was a politician, his enemies probably thought they would
have no trouble coming up with some wickedness in his personal
or professional life, right? Much to their dismay, "they could find

no charge or fault, because he was faithful; nor was there any error or fault found in him" (verse 4).

In their last-resort effort to destroy Daniel, these men said, "We shall not find any charge against this Daniel unless we find it against him concerning the law of his God" (verse 5). In other words, they would trump up charges against him by finding something "wrong" about his actions as a follower of God.

Daniel's integrity was placed on display as a result of the scrutiny of these jealous men. Integrity will stand up under the careful examination of those who attempt to bring a charge against it. As was the case with Samuel, Daniel's integrity centered on his focus on God.

The apostle Paul—On his way back to Jerusalem at the end of his third missionary journey, Paul stopped at a seaport called Miletus. There he asked the leaders from the church at Ephesus to join him for a brief visit.

First Paul gave them encouragement (see Acts 20:13-32). Then he reminded them of his conduct during the three years he spent with them, saying,

> I have coveted no one's silver or gold or apparel. Yes, you yourselves know that these hands have provided for my necessities, and for those who were with me. I have shown you in every way, by laboring like this, that you must support the weak. And remember the words of the Lord Jesus, that He said, "It is more blessed to give than to receive" (verses 33-35).

Paul led by example. He didn't ask anything of others that he would not do himself.

Shining the Spotlight on Nehemiah's Integrity

And now for Nehemiah! Now that you understand more about the awesome quality of integrity and why it's so vital and powerful in a leader, let's see how integrity was fleshed out in Nehemiah's life.

Nehemiah's time in Judea was a labor of love toward its people. In fact, it was his concern for the people that first drew him to rebuild the wall. The problem of the rich charging the poor outrageous interest on monetary loans prompted Nehemiah to defend his own conduct during his 12-year term as governor. Unlike his predecessors, he had not governed out of greed. He placed the building of the wall and the welfare of the people above his personal interests and comfort. By sharing his wealth with many on a daily basis, he set an example for the people. What does a man with integrity, a man like Nehemiah, look like?

He is selfless—During his 12-year tenure (445–432 BC), neither Nehemiah nor his kinsmen ever ate the governor's food allowance (5:14). Obviously, God had provided Nehemiah with wealth from his position as cupbearer. But Nehemiah was not greedy or desirous of increasing his own wealth at the expense of the less fortunate.

He is sensitive—Nehemiah had spent his entire life in public service, so he had seen the abuse of power and how it oppresses. Because of his reverence for God, he determined to be sensitive to the needs of others. He observed that "the former governors who were before me laid burdens on the people, and took from them bread and wine, besides forty shekels of silver. Yes, even their servants bore rule over the people, but I did not do so, because of the fear of God" (verse 15).

He is a servant—As the king's official representative, Governor Nehemiah and his men could have lorded their authority over the people. At the very least, they could have "supervised." Instead, Nehemiah and his associates served and worked on the wall alongside the citizens. Wherever a servant is, he is there to serve—not to line his own pockets at the expense of the people. Nor did Nehemiah take advantage of others by using his considerable wealth to buy up cheap land around Jerusalem (verse 16).

He is sacrificial—Nehemiah never demanded special privileges on account of his position or stature. On a daily basis, he fed—at his own table and at his personal expense—150 Jewish people and officials, not to mention "those who came to us from the nations around us." Every day an enormous quantity of food was consumed at the governor's house—an ox, six sheep, birds, and wine. And because the burden on the people was already heavy, he did not demand the food allowance to which he was entitled (verses 17-18).

He seeks only good—Nehemiah sought only the praise of God and not that of man. In all his years of service, he prayed that God would remember the good he had done for this people. Thus Nehemiah's actions were spiritually motivated, and not done for purely humanitarian reasons. He prayed, "Remember me, my God, for good, according to all that I have done for this people" (verse 19).

NEHEMIAH ON LEADERSHIP

For Nehemiah, integrity was a heart issue. And that's the secret of integrity—it's an inside job! Integrity is a matter of the heart: "A good man out of the good treasure of his heart brings forth good" (Luke 6:45). There are no "partial percentages" of integrity. Either you have it...or you don't. You are either a man of integrity...or not.

How can you make sure that integrity is alive and well in your heart and therefore your life? Here are some steps for living with integrity, which in turn, will strengthen your leadership.

Step #1: *Realize the value of integrity.* Integrity defines who you are as a leader. It also refines you and guides your actions. It puts a wall of protection around you and keeps you walking down the correct path—God's path. A wise leader highly values his integrity.

> *The end is never as satisfying as the journey.*
> *To have achieved everything but to have done so*
> *without integrity is to have achieved nothing.*
> —SOURCE UNKNOWN

Step #2: *Choose and use the truths of Scripture as your standard of integrity.* Stand with the kind of resolve shown by Martin Luther: "I am bound by the Scriptures...My conscience is captive to the

Word of God. I cannot and will not recant anything, since it is neither safe nor right to go against conscience."

Step #3: *Examine your heart.* Go to God regularly with a desire to have the searchlight of His Spirit examine your heart. Don't trust your own heart self-examination. Only God can give you a correct reading of the condition of your heart. "The heart is deceitful above all things, and desperately wicked; who can know it?" (Jeremiah 17:9). Therefore cry out to God, "Examine me, O LORD, and prove me; try my mind and my heart. Your lovingkindness is before my eyes, and I have walked in Your truth" (Psalm 26:2-3).

Step #4: *Evaluate your daily decisions.* Cautiously and prayerfully appraise your every decision, however large or small. Take time to carefully look at your choices, and then based on the truths of Scripture, decide what you must do or change in your behavior to align your life more closely to God's standards. Weigh each decision before moving ahead: Does this choice affirm my integrity? If not, obviously it's out! Have the same resolve as David: "Let the words of my mouth and the meditation of my heart be acceptable in Your sight, O LORD, my strength and my Redeemer" (Psalm 19:14).

As a leader, integrity should be at the very core of your being. Open your heart to God and let Him shape you with His Word. Then allow the Holy Spirit to guide and guard your every thought and decision, thus validating your leadership. The strength of your leadership depends on the strength of your integrity. Someone may take your life, but they cannot ever take your integrity. Only you can relinquish your integrity. So stand guard over your integrity at all costs! Live your life so you can pray, "Vindicate me, O LORD, for I have walked in my integrity. I have also trusted in the LORD; I shall not slip" (Psalm 26:1).

A person is not given integrity.
It results from the relentless pursuit
of honesty at all times.

—SOURCE UNKNOWN

16

Purity...Blesses Your Leadership

Remember me, O my God, for good!

(NEHEMIAH 13:31).

*I**t was a night much like this,* Nehemiah thought as he looked up at fading sunlight at the day's end.

And I believe this is almost the exact spot where I first scouted the broken-down wall those many years ago. He couldn't be certain it was the same spot because, as he slowly turned and took in a full panoramic view of Jerusalem, he noted the landscape had changed drastically. No longer were there mounds of rubble beneath his feet. No longer was the blessed city of God vacant of proud, secure residents. No longer was the city of David held in reproach by its neighbors. No longer were the Jewish people viewed by their enemies with disdain, as being weak and defenseless. The surrounding nations were now showing a greater level of respect. All of what he saw was good.

Nehemiah leaned against the stones of the now completed wall. As he gazed up at the twilight sky, he couldn't help but think about the fact he was now in his twilight years. He wondered, *Exactly what has been accomplished?* He could see with his own eyes that the scene around him had changed physically. The wall was complete. With that came a definite sense of safety and security. There was also evidence that the city and its people were prospering.

Nehemiah's time of reflection continued. *Have I really done all that I could have done?* His thoughts kept nagging at him. *Was I a good example of godliness for the people? I tried to live a life of purity, even though, as God knows, it wasn't always easy!*

Nehemiah shook his head as he remembered his position as governor and the many times he was approached with opportunities to compromise God's standards. The leaders who came before him had compromised, so why didn't he do the same? It would have been "normal" to give in. In fact, it was almost as if compromise was expected of one in his office!

But no! he protested. *Praise God, I resisted the temptations.*

Then he considered the possibility that his exemplary life was the reason he had been able to so strongly exhort the people to a higher level of righteousness. *I wasn't asking anything of the people that I wasn't already doing in my own life.*

Yes, the people had responded. And, yes, renewal had taken place. But it was obvious that after the wall was completed and Nehemiah had returned to the king in Susa, some things had reverted to their old state. So it was good that he had returned to Jerusalem. It looked like, once again, he was going to have to deal with people who were living in sin and had compromised their Jewish heritage during his absence.

Nehemiah then wondered, *Are the doubts I'm feeling due to the weariness of my body, or is it the enemy of my soul that is causing this uncertainty?* Finally, after struggling over this for a while, he did what he had always done when there was a battle raging in his heart and mind: He prayed! "Remember me, O my God, for good!"

God's Standard of Purity

As you've worked your way through this book, you've seen many qualities about Nehemiah that made him a strong leader. Most of these qualities are essential to effective leadership. But as we come to the end of the book of Nehemiah it's time for us to take a last look at the man and discover the trait that was the most essential for leading others.

God says that His leader—whether of few or a multitude—must be obedient. That person must be one "who will do all My will" (Acts 13:22). God's leader is submissive to God's leading. He desires to do what God asks of him. And what does God ask of His leaders? He asks them—and you—to follow His standard for purity.

God set the standard of purity—During the early days of the forma- tion of the new nation of Israel, God often had to remind all the people, including Moses and the leaders, that "I am the LORD your God. You shall therefore consecrate yourselves, and you shall be holy; for I am holy" (Leviticus 11:44). God's standard back then was holiness, and that's true for today as well. Nehemiah set the stan- dard, and he expected everyone to adhere to it, especially his coleaders. They were expected to model purity before the people.

Jesus affirmed the standard of purity—Jesus verbalized the Father's desire for purity in his people, regardless of rank or privilege, when He declared, "You shall be perfect, just as your Father in heaven is perfect" (Matthew 5:48). It stands to reason that a holy God can accept nothing less than a holy people.

Jesus made the standard of purity attainable—What the Father and the Son were asking of their followers was impossible for anyone to attain. So, what did God do to make the standard achievable? In the Old Testament God's standard was for the people to offer ani- mal sacrifices. And the blood from these sacrifices would symboli- cally cover the sins of the people and their leaders.

But the New Testament message of the gospel changed all that. With Jesus' death came the payment for sin and a chance to take on purity: "He [God] made Him [Jesus] who knew no sin to be sin for us, that we might become the righteousness [purity] of God in Him [Jesus]" (2 Corinthians 5:21).

Jesus asks His leaders to walk in purity—If you are a believer in Jesus, you have His purity, His righteousness, dwelling within you. That means you can choose to live out the purity that resides in you. The apostle Paul pointed to this choice in one of his prayers to believers:

"We…do not cease to pray for you, and to ask that…you may walk worthy of the Lord, fully pleasing Him" (Colossians 1:9-10).

Paul's reference to walking worthy is his description of how you and all believers can live out God's standard of purity on a daily, step-by-step, decision-by-decision basis. This means choosing to walk by the Spirit (Galatians 5:22-23) rather than being controlled by our passions. As those who possess the Holy Spirit, we can choose to put our old passions and desires to death. Since "we live in the Spirit, let us also walk in the Spirit" (Galatians 5:25).

Jesus asks His leaders to model purity—Leadership is influence. One man can lead others only to the extent that he can influence them. Any leader, including one of God's leaders, can influence others to varying degrees by his personality, ability to persuade, or personal power. But it is personal godliness that has the greatest bearing on the extent of our influence.

In the Bible, this essential leadership trait is described as being "blameless" (1 Timothy 3:2; Titus 1:6) or "above reproach" (NASB). In other words, the life of God's man is an open book. No charge can be laid against him or his character. His example makes it possible for him to influence others. This doesn't mean he is sinless, but rather, he is striving for purity in his daily life. The goal is to be free from public accusation and scandal. His desire for purity is what gives him strength as a leader. That's why personal purity is so important, why confession of sin is so essential. A leader after God's own heart needs to keep short records with God (1 John 1:9).

Setting the Stage

A focus on purity sets the stage perfectly for our final chapter on the life of the great leader Nehemiah. He knew what all God's men need to learn: A leader who is pure is a leader who is blessed and blesses others. He knew that a lack of purity would hinder his influence. So beginning with his first recorded prayer, Nehemiah made sure to confess his sins as well as the sins of his fellow Jews:

> Please let Your ear be attentive and Your eyes open, that You may hear the prayer of Your servant which I pray before You now, day and night, for the children of Israel Your servants, and confess the sins of the children of Israel which we have sinned against You. Both my father's house and I have sinned. We have acted very corruptly against You, and have not kept the commandments, the statutes, nor the ordinances which You commanded Your servant Moses (Nehemiah 1:6-7).

During the years of Nehemiah's first administration, things ran smoothly. The opposition in Jerusalem could do little to rise up against such a capable leader and administrator. His very life was a model of purity. Using a term that appears in the New Testament, he was "above reproach" (Titus 1:6 NASB).

While Nehemiah led the people in Jerusalem and provided hands-on leadership, the people conformed to the covenants they had made with God and lived relatively prosperous and uneventful lives. But after Nehemiah finished serving as governor, he returned to the court of Artaxerxes in Babylon, where he remained for "certain days" (13:6). With Nehemiah gone, things began to take a turn for the worse in Jerusalem.

It is unknown exactly how long Nehemiah remained in Persia, but it was long enough for disobedience to develop among the people back in Israel. During his absence, the opposition party worked overtime to overturn Nehemiah's influence.

In time, however, Nehemiah returned as governor of Judah. Upon his arrival, it was obvious that the people had reverted to impurity and forsaken the temple and its worship. By this time, sin had found its way into all levels of society.

Nehemiah Confronted Impurity

When the standard for spiritual leaders is on a par with whatever is acceptable to the people, spiritual anarchy is sure to prevail. Sadly, this was God's charge against the ten northern tribes of Israel not too long before they were sent into exile in 722 BC. In Hosea 4:9, God announced, "Like people, like priest. So I will punish them for their ways." God judged these people and sent them into exile, never to be heard of again.

When Nehemiah returned to Jerusalem he found that a similar spiritual decline had taken place—even after all the struggles and triumphs and advancements he had made during his previous stay. He now had to confront the impurity of the people from their leaders on down. Here is a short list of the sins he discovered on his return:

The problem of compromise (Nehemiah 13:4-9). The people—and especially the leaders—had allowed foreigners like the Ammonites and Moabites to participate in their assembly. Eliashib, the high priest, has even given Tobiah, one of the chief antagonists of Nehemiah, a room in the temple!

The problem of withholding (13:10-14). Nehemiah's next investigation revealed that the tithes had not been regularly collected. The result? The temple workers (the Levites) were not given their portion of the offerings and were forced to return to their lands to provide for their families. Therefore, the temple and its upkeep was neglected.

The problem of the Sabbath (13:15-22). The Sabbath was not being observed. The people were treating the Sabbath day like any other business day, filling it with buying, selling, trading, and personal interests.

The problem of domestic disobedience (13:23-28). The Jewish men had married foreign wives. The most brazen illustration of this violation of God's law was the grandson of the high priest, Eliashib. He had married a daughter of Sanballat, the governor of Samaria, an enemy of the Jews.

Nehemiah Demanded Purity

Because Nehemiah had sought to live a life of purity, he had earned the right to deal forcefully with the widespread impurity he observed in Jerusalem. Therefore he faced each problem head-on. Purity doesn't compromise, and it doesn't come in degrees. It is all or nothing. The spiritual leaders in Jerusalem were participating in sin and, as a result, allowing sinful behavior to permeate the people. Nehemiah dove in and dealt with each problem directly and, at times, drastically. Here's how he handled the four main problems already listed.

Compromise (13:4-9)—"I threw all the household goods of Tobiah out of the room. Then I commanded them to cleanse the rooms in the temple" (verses 8-9).

Withholding (13:10-14)—"I contended with the rules, and said, 'Why is the house of God forsaken?' And I gathered them together and set them in their place." Then Nehemiah appointed fiscal managers who "were considered faithful, and their task was to distribute to their brethren" (verses 11,14). This enabled the Levites to return to their duties in the temple.

The Sabbath (13:15-22)—"Then I contended with the nobles of Judah, and said to them, 'What evil thing is this that you do, by which you profane the Sabbath day?'...I commanded the gates to be shut, and charged that they must not be opened till after the Sabbath. Then I posted some of my servants at the gates" (verses 17,19).

Domestic disobedience (13:23-28)—"So I contended with them and cursed them, struck some of them and pulled out their hair, and made them swear by God, saying, 'You shall not give your daughters as wives to their sons, nor take their daughters for your sons or yourselves.' Therefore I drove him [the son-in-law of Sanballat] from me" (verses 25,28).

Purity and the Blessings of God

I hope you recall how we first met Nehemiah. Beginning with

Crisis #1 in Nehemiah chapter 1, we have witnessed him as a man of prayer, and this is the case throughout the 13 chapters that make up the book of Nehemiah. We first observed Nehemiah on his knees acknowledging his own sin and the sins of his people (1:6). In that prayer he also asked for God's blessing as he expressed his desire to be obedient to God's will.

Now, in the last verse in the last chapter of the book of Nehemiah, we again see him on his knees desiring the same thing of God—God's blessing on his life and the lives of the people. God answered both of Nehemiah's prayers. His leadership was blessed from start to finish. And God blessed him with the wisdom needed to direct the people spiritually so God could bless them.

Steps to Purity

If you desire God's blessings on your life and your leadership, then purity must be your top priority. A leader after God's own heart is not perfect, but he is progressing. Purity for you, God's man, is to be a constant desire. Purity will fortify your leadership if you will take the following steps:

Step #1—Look into your heart. Hopefully you'll see a man who, although not perfect, is at least trying to improve, a man who's moving steadily toward God's standards. Ask God what David asked: "Examine me, O LORD, and prove me; try my mind and my heart" (Psalm 26:2).

Step #2—Deal with sin. Sin is anything that is contrary to the will of God. To sin is to miss the mark with God. And with God, the standard is perfection. Therefore, everyone has sin to deal with. As the apostle John noted, "If we say that we have no sin, we deceive ourselves." Instead, he said we are to "confess our sins," knowing that "He is faithful and just to forgive us our sins and to cleanse us from all unrighteousness" (1 John 1:8-9).

Step #3—Develop personal convictions. To keep from being stained and sidetracked by the world, you must develop some bold spiritual convictions about what you believe. This strong shield of faith will protect you from the "fiery darts of the wicked one" (Ephesians 6:16) and give you courage to stand up for your convictions and resist the temptation to sin. "Submit to God. Resist the devil and he will flee from you" (James 4:7).

Step #4—Temper your convictions with compassion. You, as a leader after God's own heart, need to realize that most people aren't where you are spiritually. In fact, as you already know, you are not where you want to be when it comes to purity! Paul advises, "If a man is overtaken in any trespass, you who are spiritual restore such a one in a spirit of gentleness, considering yourself lest you also be tempted. Bear one another's burdens, and so fulfill the law of Christ" (Galatians 6:1-2).

NEHEMIAH ON LEADERSHIP

Nehemiah's life—and his purity—caused him to suffer greatly at the hands of both his enemies and his own people. That is the downside of purity. However, his godly standard allowed him to lead others in the way of holiness as a leader after God's own heart.

Nehemiah prayed that his labors and sacrifices were not in vain. And God answered his prayer. His life did count. Things did change in his own generation. And history records his reforms continued into the next generation. He did his part, and God immortalized his efforts in the book of the Bible that bears his name. God did remember Nehemiah, and so do we.

Nehemiah asked God to bless his efforts and that he be remembered for good. What are you asking God to remember about your life? On the spiritual level, what has your leadership accomplished for God and His people? If you have a family, what effect has your leadership had on them? Are there changes you need to make?

And how about your everyday work life? How has your leadership contributed to the good of others? If your spiritual inventory has brought you up a little short and there hasn't been a lot for you to be remembered by, then ask God to show you a new purpose for your life. Ask Him to help you live a life of

> strength,
>
> purity,
>
> prayer,
>
> wisdom,
>
> courage,
>
> and spiritual growth.

Live for the good of others with all your heart, soul, body, mind, and strength. Pray Nehemiah's heart-prayer today: "Remember me, O my God, for good!"

> *The true spiritual leader is concerned infinitely*
> *more with the service he can render God and*
> *his fellow-men than with the benefits and*
> *pleasures he can extract from life. He aims to*
> *put more into life than he takes out of it.*[40]

STUDY GUIDE

1

STRENGTH...GOD'S PROMISE FOR YOUR LEADERSHIP

As we start our study of *A Leader After God's Own Heart*, jot down what you have read or heard about Nehemiah.

How do you respond to the question "Who, me? A leader?"

Thinking about God's promise of strength found in Philippians 4:13, write down some concerns you have in your "all things" category (for example, family, witness, work, personal purity).

Now, take these concerns to God and ask Him for strength to deal with these issues!

How serious have you been in the past about abiding in Christ?

What steps can you take to improve on your relationship with Jesus?

What steps can you take to be more accountable to others?

Look at the list in the section entitled "Exercise Your Faith." Pick out one item in the list and state what you can do to grow in this area.

What one truth from the "Nehemiah on Leadership" section spoke to you, and why?

STUDY GUIDE

2

CRISIS MANAGEMENT...DRAWS OUT YOUR LEADERSHIP

Read Nehemiah 1:1-3, then describe the crisis Nehemiah faced and why it had such a grave effect on him.

Relate a crisis you have faced. Were you more concerned about the problem it presented to you, or the effect it would have on others?

How does former President Kennedy's description of the word *crisis*—with reference to the Chinese characters used for the word— help you to see crises in a different light?

What part of Nehemiah's response to his crisis did you find helpful as you deal with your own crisis?

Describe what Johnson & Johnson did right in their crisis management.

What about Exxon's crisis management?

What one truth from the "Nehemiah on Leadership" section spoke to you, and why?

3

PRAYER...EMPOWERS YOUR LEADERSHIP

Read Nehemiah 1:4-11. Describe Nehemiah's attitude as he entered into prayer (verse 4).

How long did this attitude persist (verse 4)?

According to *A Leader After God's Own Heart*, how long did Nehemiah pray?

Make a list of the characteristics of Nehemiah's prayer (praise, earnestness, etc.). Which of these characteristics of prayer do you find the easiest to practice?

Which do you find the most difficult?

Read the story of Hezekiah's confrontation with the king of Assyria in 2 Kings 18:9–19:37.

Why was Hezekiah offended when he received King Sennacherib's letter?

What was Hezekiah's response?

What lessons does Hezekiah's conduct teach you about how you should respond to what's happening around you?

Past great leaders have been men of prayer. Are you exposed to any modern-day leaders who pray? What is your reaction to seeing them pray? How could their example be a source of strength for your own prayer life?

What one truth from the "Nehemiah on Leadership" section spoke to you, and why?

STUDY GUIDE

COURAGE...SOLIDIFIES
YOUR LEADERSHIP

Read Nehemiah 1:11–2:3. What was Nehemiah's reaction to the king's observation? What did Nehemiah then do?

How should a leader deal with his emotions? Are there times when a leader can and should show his emotions?

Read again the words Martin Luther spoke in courage, and compare his level of spiritual courage to yours.

Read Joshua chapter 1 and count the number of times God used the word "courage" in His exhortation to Joshua.

How does this chapter encourage you with regard to your fears?

What one truth from the "Nehemiah on Leadership" section spoke to you, and why?

WISDOM...PROMOTES
YOUR LEADERSHIP

Read Nehemiah 2:4-9. How do these verses speak of Nehemiah's wisdom? Read James 1:5 and answer the following questions:

What word in the verse alerts you that wisdom doesn't come automatically?

What can you do when you find that your wisdom is in short supply?

How freely does God give His wisdom?

What's His attitude as He gives it?

What promise are you given with regard to seeking wisdom?

What's the difference between wisdom and knowledge?

Describe the different ways you can obtain wisdom.

Reread the section "Nehemiah's Life of Wisdom." List below the first three words in each paragraph that describes Nehemiah's wisdom. Then select one item from the list that you would like to work on this week. What first step could you take?

What one truth from the "Nehemiah on Leadership" section spoke to you, and why?

PLANNING...BRINGS FOCUS TO YOUR LEADERSHIP

Read Nehemiah 2:4-9, then review the section entitled "Qualities of an Effective Planner." Share your thoughts on how Nehemiah displayed each of these qualities:

Passion—

Support—

Clear-cut objective—

A time frame—

Permission—

Acquisition—

Provision—

Could Nehemiah have lacked any of these qualities and still have gotten the job done well? Which qualities, and why?

See the section entitled "Two Types of People." When it comes to planning, are you a Type 1 person or a Type 2 person?

In terms of planning ahead, describe how you approached a recent project.

Based on what happened with that recent project, what could you have done better in your planning?

Do you agree that planning ahead will get you ahead? Why or why not?

Based on your observations of other people, what results have you seen come from a failure to plan ahead?

What one truth from the "Nehemiah on Leadership" section spoke to you, and why?

MOTIVATION...EXTENDS YOUR LEADERSHIP

Read Nehemiah 2:11-20. Why do you think Nehemiah took a secret tour of the broken-down wall before he spoke to the people?

Now describe Nehemiah's approach and its result.

Describe your usual style for motivating others. Is it externally or internally inspired/derived?

How can you get a person who likes the status quo to move forward? (Assume that forward motion is a good thing!)

What are your thoughts about your role as a "change agent"?

Do you agree or disagree that motivation begins with you?

Circle the phrase below that best describes your level of self-motivation.

Not a self-starter.

Sometimes takes initiative.

Works hard at being a self-starter.

Quickly review the section entitled "Motivation Starts with You." Circle, in your book, the challenges that might help you become more self-motivated. Pick out several and explain here how each challenge would help you become more self-motivated.

Describe how motivation can extend your leadership.

What one truth from the "Nehemiah on Leadership" section spoke to you, and why?

DELEGATION...UNLEASHES
YOUR LEADERSHIP

Starting at verse 1, read through Nehemiah chapter 3, then describe Nehemiah's strategy for rebuilding the wall.

In Exodus 18, what advice did Jethro give to his son-in-law?

Reread the section "The Fear of Delegation." Which fears cause you to hesitate in your delegation, and why?

What was Jesus' strategy for spreading the gospel message?

What was the apostle Paul's strategy for delegation, according to Ephesians 4:11-12?

Refresh your memory of Nehemiah's ability to delegate by finishing this acrostic:

D–

E–

L–

E–

G–

A–

T–

E–

Do you agree with Theodore Roosevelt's quote? Why or why not?

What one truth from the "Nehemiah on Leadership" section spoke to you, and why?

ENCOURAGEMENT...
SUPPORTS YOUR LEADERSHIP

Read Nehemiah 4. Now look at your own life as a leader either in your family, or at church, or at your workplace. What encouragement have you recently offered in any of your roles?

Who could you have encouraged but didn't? How can you remedy that?

Is there anyone you can think of who may need some words of encouragement from you today?

When you think of encouragement, which person comes to mind and why?

Relate a time when you were discouraged. How did you overcome the discouragement?

Review the section entitled "Reasons for Discouragement." What are the warning signs that discouragement might be creeping into your life?

Why is discouragement potentially catastrophic in the life of a leader (hint: discouragement is contagious)?

Look at the section entitled "Dealing with Discouragement." What two or three suggestions stand out to you right now, and why?

What one truth from the "Nehemiah on Leadership" section spoke to you, and why?

PROBLEM-SOLVING...
REFINES YOUR LEADERSHIP

Read Nehemiah 5:1-13. What was happening?

Have you ever had to deal with the problem of "the enemy within"? If so, how did you resolve it? If not, state why this might be a major problem for any leader.

Internal strife is only one of many possible problems you might be facing today. What is your #1 problem? State it here:

It has been said, "A problem defined is half solved." Now that you have defined your #1 problem, what next step might you take to solve it?

After reading about the way Moses' brother, Aaron, handled the Israelites' request to make an idol, what are your thoughts about the dangers of taking the easy way out when solving a problem?

Comment on the statement, "Problem solving is one of the hardest tasks a leader faces." Do you agree or disagree? Explain.

What one truth from the "Nehemiah on Leadership" section spoke to you, and why?

CONFLICT MANAGEMENT...GIVES RESOLVE TO YOUR LEADERSHIP

Read Nehemiah 6. What was Nehemiah's attitude as he faced each conflict?

How would you differentiate between a problem and a conflict?

Could both a problem and a conflict be handled in a similar manner? Why or why not?

When facing your own conflicts, how have you been challenged by...

   Ridicule?

   Threats?

   Diversion?

Slander?

Treachery?

Which of the above challenges was the most difficult for you, and why?

Which suggestion(s) from "Leadership and Conflict Management" did you find the most helpful, and why?

What one truth from the "Nehemiah on Leadership" section spoke to you, and why?

VISION...GIVES DIRECTION TO YOUR LEADERSHIP

Read Nehemiah 2:5. What was Nehemiah's request?

Read through Nehemiah 11 until you are ready to jot a brief description of what was happening here:

How does this fulfill Nehemiah's vision toward the city of Jerusalem?

In your personal life, why is the future important?

In your business life, why is the future important?

In your family life, why is the future important?

Read the story of Joshua and Caleb in Numbers 13. What set them apart from the other ten spies?

A key element of being a strong leader is having a vision for the future. State one of your key visions or dreams here (whether it has to do with your family, your workplace, etc.).

Review the section entitled "A Vision's Key Features" and answer the following questions:

A vision must be felt deeply. How strongly do you feel about this dream or idea?

A vision must be shared. Who can you share it with?

A vision must inspire. Restate your idea or dream in a way that someone else could see its value.

A vision must unify. Who would be negatively affected by your dream? Who would it divide (your family, your company, etc.)?

A vision must be repeated. Who may have forgotten about your great idea? Maybe it's time to remind them!

What one truth from the "Nehemiah on Leadership" section spoke to you, and why?

RENEWAL...REFRESHES YOUR LEADERSHIP

Read Nehemiah 8:1-18. Describe the request the Jews made of Ezra (verse 1).

What does this tell you about their "felt" need?

Why do you think there was such a hunger of heart?

What do Nehemiah 8:13 and 8:18 tell you about the sincerity of their request?

Under the section entitled "Everyone Needs Renewal," which ideas might you find beneficial? List as many as you can, and state why they would help you.

Read Romans 12:2. Using a dictionary, write out a definition for the word "conform."

Then using the meaning of "conform," restate how God would want you to respond to the secular world around you.

What does the psalmist say about the Bible's ability to work in your life?

Psalm 19:7—

Psalm 19:8—

According to Hebrews 4:12, what can the Bible do in the life of a believer?

Read the section entitled "Renewal and the Word of God." Note the various signs of renewal that appeared in the lives of the Jewish people. Now take a closer look at your own spiritual life. Are there any signs that spiritual renewal is taking place? What are these signs?

No one should be totally satisfied with their spiritual condition. What steps can you take now to ensure continued spiritual renewal in your life?

What one truth from the "Nehemiah on Leadership" section spoke to you, and why?

LOYALTY...AFFIRMS
YOUR LEADERSHIP

Read Nehemiah 2:1-6. What was the king's request, and what was Nehemiah's response (verse 6)?

Read Nehemiah 13:6 and comment on Nehemiah's loyalty.

Using a dictionary, write out a definition for the word *loyalty*.

Using this definition, state your level of loyalty in the following areas of your life:

Your relationship to Jesus—

Your family—

Your friends—

Your church—

Your boss—

Review the section "Loyalty Begins with Trust." Which area of trust in God has strengthened your loyalty to God, and why?

What are some ways to promote loyalty between you and the people you work with?

In response to the section "Leaders and Loyalty," give a short statement describing your loyalty in the following areas:

Loyalty to God—

Loyalty to God's Word—

Loyalty to your superiors—

Loyalty to your work—

Loyalty to your workers—

Loyal to the end—

In the section "Inspiring Loyalty," note the areas in which you could use some improvement. Then write down one thing you can do this week to help inspire loyalty.

What one truth from the "Nehemiah on Leadership" section spoke to you, and why?

STUDY GUIDE

INTEGRITY...VALIDATES
YOUR LEADERSHIP

Read Nehemiah 5:14-19. In what ways was Nehemiah different than the leaders who preceded him?

What general principles can you discover from Nehemiah's actions that could help you strengthen your integrity as a leader?

Integrity made a difference in the life of Martin Luther. He was willing to die for his beliefs. In what areas of your life do you need to exhibit a greater level of integrity? List them, and then ask God to give you the conviction to stand firm!

Read again the section entitled "The Meaning of Integrity." Then look up the word *integrity* in a dictionary, and, in your own words, describe it.

What insights do you gain about the character of integrity in the section entitled "The Nature of Integrity"?

Read 1 Samuel 12:1-5 and briefly describe Samuel's testimony to his integrity.

Read Daniel 6:1-17 and briefly note the ways in which Daniel showed integrity.

Read Acts 20:33-35 and describe the apostle Paul's conduct toward the Ephesians.

What one truth from the "Nehemiah on Leadership" section spoke to you, and why?

PURITY...BLESSES
YOUR LEADERSHIP

Read Nehemiah 1:4-11, then read Daniel 9:3-11. Why do you think God blessed the lives and ministries of these two great men?

Read Nehemiah 13:4-28 and describe some of the problems Nehemiah faced when he returned to Jerusalem for a second tour as governor:

Why would purity be a source of strength as Nehemiah dealt with these problems?

Read Acts 13:22 and describe how purity intersects with this verse.

Review the section "God's Standard of Purity" and describe the progression of purity from God the Father through Jesus to you the leader and your example to your followers.

What are your thoughts about your example? What might you do to become a better example?

How would you evaluate your willingness to take the following steps toward greater purity?

Step #1—Take an honest look at your own heart.

Step #2—Deal with sin.

Step #3—Develop personal convictions.

Step #4—Temper your convictions with compassion.

What one truth from the "Nehemiah on Leadership" section spoke to you, and why?

Having now read and completed all the study questions, what two ideas, principles, suggestions, or admonitions did you find most helpful that you could put into practice today or this week?

Takeaway truth #1?

Takeaway truth #2?

BIBLIOGRAPHY

Axelrod, Alan. *Patton on Leadership*. Paramus, NJ: Prentice Hall Press, 1999.

Barber, Cyril J. *Nehemiah and the Dynamics of Effective Leadership*. Neptune, NJ: Loizeaux Brothers, 1976.

Boa, Kenneth, Sid Buzzell, and Bill Perkins. *Handbook to Leadership*. Atlanta, GA: Trinity House, 2007.

Buzzell, Sid, gen. ed. *The Leadership Bible*. Grand Rapids, MI: Zondervan, 1998.

Campbell, Donald K. *Nehemiah: Man in Charge*. Wheaton, IL: Victor Books, 1979.

Chambers, Oswald. *Christian Disciplines*. Grand Rapids, MI: Discovery House, 1995.

Crocker III, H.W. *Robert E. Lee on Leadership*. Roseville, CA: Prima Publishing, 2000.

Engstrom, Ted W. *Motivation to Last a Lifetime*. Grand Rapids, MI: Zondervan, 1984.

Engstrom, Ted W. and Edward R. Dayton. *The Art of Management for Christian Leaders*. Waco, TX: Word Books, 1978.

Finzel, Hans. *The Top Ten Mistakes Leaders Make*. Colorado Springs, CO: NexGen, 2000.

Freeman, James M. *Manners and Customs of the Bible*. Plainfield, NJ: Logos International, 1972.

George, Jim. *The Bare Bones Bible Handbook*. Eugene, OR: Harvest House, 2006.

George, Jim. *The Remarkable Prayers of the Bible*. Eugene, OR: Harvest House, 2005.

George, Jim. *What God Wants to Do for You*. Eugene, OR: Harvest House, 2004.

Gitomer, Jeffrey. *Jeffrey Gitomer's Little Book of Leadership*. Hoboken, NJ: John Wiley & Sons, Inc., 2011.

Matthews, Victor H. *Manners and Customs in the Bible*. Peabody, MA: Hendrickson, 1991.

Maxwell, John C. *The 21 Indispensable Qualities of a Leader*. Nashville, TN: Thomas Nelson, 1999.

Maxwell, John C. *The 21 Most Powerful Minutes in a Leader's Day*. Nashville, TN: Thomas Nelson, 2000.

Maxwell, John C., exec. ed. *The Maxwell Leadership Bible*. Nashville, TN: Thomas Nelson, 2002.

Peters, Thomas J., and Robert H. Waterman, Jr. *In Search of Excellence*. New York: Harper Collins, 1982.

Phillips, Donald T. *Lincoln on Leadership*. New York: Warner Books, 1993.

Safire, William, and Leonard Safir, eds. *Leadership: A Treasury of Great Quotations for Those Who Aspire to Lead.* New York: Galahad Books, 1990.

Sanders, J. Oswald. *Spiritual Leadership.* Chicago, IL: Moody Press, 1967.

Seume, Richard H. *Nehemiah: God's Builder.* Chicago, IL: Moody Press, 1978.

Spence, H.D.M., and Joseph S. Exell. *The Pulpit Commentary, Volume 7—Ezra, Nehemiah, Esther & Job.* Grand Rapids, MI: Eerdmans, 1978.

Swindoll, Charles R. *Hand Me Another Brick.* Nashville, TN: Thomas Nelson, 1978.

Wight, Fred H. *Manners and Customs of Bible Lands.* Chicago, IL: Moody Press, 1978.

NOTES

1. In a speech by John F. Kennedy (1959), as cited in *The Merriam-Webster Dictionary of Quotations* (Springfield, MA: Merriam-Webster), p. 81.

2. Thomas J. Peters and Robert H Waterman, Jr., *In Search of Excellence* (New York: HarperCollins, 1982). See the chapter titled "Back to Basics."

3. In Cyril J. Barber, *Nehemiah and the Dynamics of Effective Leadership* (Neptune, NJ: Loizeaux Brothers, 1976), p. 24.

4. Hans Finzel, *The Top Ten Mistakes Leaders Make* (Colorado Springs, CO: Cook Communications Ministries, 2000), p. 39.

5. J. Oswald Sanders, *Spiritual Leadership* (Chicago IL: Moody Press, 1967), p. 122.

6. Written by Jean Klett, a business coach and mentor who assists serious entrepreneurs in building a profitable online business with multiple income streams. Published July 5, 2009. For more information and to contact the author, go to: http://www.7figurelifeplan.com.

7. Ibid.

8. Charles R. Swindoll, *Hand Me Another Brick* (Nashville TN: Thomas Nelson, 1978), p. 41.

9. In J. Oswald Sanders, *Spiritual Leadership* (Chicago, IL: Moody Press, 1967), p. 84.

10. At www.1-famous-quotes.com/quote/38977.

11. Herbert Lockyer, *All the Prayers of the Bible* (Grand Rapids: Zondervan, 1973), see the section on Nehemiah.

12. J. Sidlow Baxter, http://en.wikiquote.org/wiki/J._Sidlow_Baxter.

13. John C. Maxwell, *The 21 Indispensable Qualities of a Leader* (Nashville, TN: Thomas Nelson, 1999), p. 41.

14. J. Oswald Sanders, *Spiritual Leadership*, quoting James Burn, *Revivals, Their Laws and Leaders* (Chicago IL: Moody Press, 1979), pp. 181-82.

15. H.W. Crocker III, *Robert E. Lee on Leadership—Executive Lessons in Character, Courage, and Vision* (Roseville, CA: Prima Publishing, 2000), p. 35.

16. Kenneth Boa, Sid Buzzell, and Bill Perkins, *Handbook to Leadership* (Atlanta, GA: Trinity House, 2007), p. 178.

17. Ted W. Engstrom, *The Making of a Christian Leader* (Grand Rapids: Zondervan, 1976), p. 141.

18. Edwin Bliss, *Getting Things Done* (New York: Bantam, 1984), p. 127.

19. General Dwight D. Eisenhower and 34th President of the United States is credited with saying this.

20. Ted W. Engstrom, *The Making of a Christian Leader* (Grand Rapids: Zondervan, 1976), p. 134.

21. Donald K. Campbell, *Nehemiah: Man in Charge* (Wheaton, IL: Victor, 1979), p. 21.

22. Ted W. Engstrom, *Motivation to Last a Lifetime* (Grand Rapids: Zondervan, 1984), p. 92.

23. At www.brainyquote.com/quote/authors/h/henry-ford.html.

24. This quote is attributed to J.C. Penny, but the source is unknown.

25. Hans Finzel, *The Top Ten Mistakes Leaders Make* (Colorado Springs CO: Cook Communications Ministries, 2000).

26. At www.juntosociety.com/uspresidents/troosevelt.html.

27. Ted W. Engstrom, *Motivation to Last a Lifetime.*

28. Michael Griffiths, *God's Forgetful Pilgrims* (Grand Rapids: Eerdmans, 1975).

29. Cyril J. Barber, *Nehemiah and the Dynamics of Effective Leadership* (Neptune, NJ: Loizeaux Brothers, 1980), p. 71.

30. Jeffrey Gitomer, *Jeffrey Gitomer's Little Book of Leadership* (Hoboken, NJ: John Wiley & Sons, 2011), p. 17.

31. Alan Axelrod, *Patton on Leadership: Strategic Lessons for Corporate Warfare* (Paramus, NJ: Prentice Hall Press, 1999), p. 185.

32. Axelrod, *Patton on Leadership*, p. 128.

33. Henry Jacobsen, *Building with God: Ezra, Nehemiah* (Wheaton IL: Scripture Press, 1968), p. 63.

34. Hans Finzel, *The Top Ten Mistakes Leaders Make* (Colorado Springs, CO: Cook Communications Ministries, 2000), p. 180.

35. J. Oswald Sanders, *Spiritual Leadership* (Chicago, IL: Moody Press, 1967), p. 48.

36. John C. Maxwell, *The Maxwell Leadership Bible* (Nashville, TN: Thomas Nelson, 2002), p. 969.

37. In J. Oswald Sanders, *Spiritual Leadership* (Chicago, IL: Moody Press, 1967), p. 115.

38. William Safire and Leonard Safir, *Leadership, A Treasury of Great Quotations for Those Who Aspire to Lead* (New York: Galahad Books, 1990), p. 134.

39. Kouzes, James M., and Posner, Barry Z., *Credibility: How Leaders Gain and Lose It, Why People Demand It* (San Francisco CA: Jossey-Bass, 2011), p. 5.

40. J. Oswald Sanders, *Spiritual Leadership* (Chicago, IL: Moody Press, 1967), p. 13.

Other Books by Jim George

The Bare Bones Bible® Handbook
The perfect resource for a fast and friendly overview of every book of the Bible. Includes the grand theme and main points of each book, the key men and women of God and what you can learn from them, the major events in Bible history, and personal applications for spiritual growth and daily living.

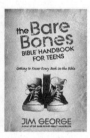

The Bare Bones Bible® Handbook for Teens
Based on the bestselling *Bare Bones Bible® Handbook,* this edition includes content and life applications specially written with teens in mind! They will be amazed at how much the Bible has to say about the things that matter most to them—their happiness, friends and family, home and school, and goals for the future. Great for youth group studies!

The Bare Bones Bible® Facts
This book brings Bible facts to life through more than 150 carefully selected topics that provide fascinating insights about important historical events, interesting customs and cultural practices, and significant people and places.

10 Minutes to Knowing the Men and Women of the Bible
The lessons you can learn from the outstanding men and women of the Bible are powerfully relevant for today. As you review their lives through the biographical sketches in this book, you'll discover special qualities worth emulating and life lessons for everyday living, which will energize your spiritual growth.

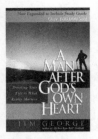

A Man After God's Own Heart

Many Christian men want to be men after God's own heart... but how do they do this? George shows that a heartfelt desire to practice God's priorities is all that's needed. God's grace does the rest. Includes study guide. This book has appeared on the Evangelical Christian Booksellers Association's bestseller list.

A Husband After God's Own Heart

Husbands will find their marriages growing richer and deeper as they pursue God and discover 12 areas in which they can make a real difference in their relationship with their wife. (This book was a 2005 Gold Medallion Award Finalist.)

The Man Who Makes a Difference

What made the apostle Paul so effective, so influential? Readers will experience true fulfillment as they learn how they can make a real and lasting difference in the workplace, at home, at church, and in their community.

A Young Man After God's Own Heart

Pursuing God really *is* an adventure—a lot like climbing a mountain. There are all kinds of challenges on the way up, but the awesome view at the top is well worth the trip. This book helps teen men to experience the thrill of knowing real success in life—the kind that counts with God. (This book was a 2006 Gold Medallion Award Finalist.)

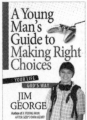

A Young Man's Guide to Making Right Choices

This book will help teen men to think carefully about their decisions, assuring a more fulfilling and successful life. A great resource for gaining the skills needed to face life's challenges.

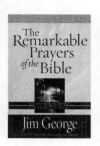

The Remarkable Prayers of the Bible

Jim looks deeply into prayers of great men and women in the Bible and shares more than a hundred practical applications that can help shape your life and prayers. A separate *Growth and Study Guide* is also available.

A Little Boy After God's Own Heart

(*coauthored with Elizabeth George*)

With delightful artwork by Judy Luenebrink, this book encourages young boys in the virtues of patience, goodness, faithfulness, sharing, and more. Written to help boys discover how special they are, these rhymes present wisdom and character traits for life.

God Loves His Precious Children

(*coauthored with Elizabeth George*)

Jim and Elizabeth George share the comfort and assurance of Psalm 23 with young children. Engaging watercolor scenes and delightful rhymes bring the truths and promises of each verse to life.

God's Wisdom for Little Boys

(*coauthored with Elizabeth George*)

The wonderful teachings of Proverbs come to life for boys. Memorable rhymes play alongside colorful paintings for an exciting presentation of truths to live by.

About the Author

Jim George is a teacher and speaker and an award-winning, bestselling author of numerous books, including *A Man After God's Own Heart* and *The Bare Bones Bible®️ Handbook*. To order any of his books, email Jim at:

www.JimGeorge.com

Jim and Elizabeth George Ministries
P.O. Box 2879
Belfair, WA 98528
1-800-542-4611